GASLIGHTING RECOVERY

How to Avoid and Recognize Manipulative

(A Step-by-step Recovery Guide to Heal From Emotional Abuse)

Leland Dillion

I0145842

Published By Regina Loviusher

Leland Dillion

All Rights Reserved

Gaslighting Recovery: How to Avoid and Recognize Manipulative (A Step-by-step Recovery Guide to Heal From Emotional Abuse)

ISBN 978-1-77485-288-0

Legal & Disclaimer

TABLE OF CONTENTS

Introduction

The term "gas lighting" refers to a form of manipulation that is used in mental abuse. The perpetrator also exposes their victims to fake information, in order they can be better understood by them. The goal of the abuser is to make their victims be concerned about their own security and their memory of a particular situation. They don't see the person who is committing the offense as doing something wrong in this manner. Gas lighting is typically done by psychopaths who have personality disorders that are characterized by an absence of remorse, and more aggressive behavior.

These personality traits enable people to manipulate others for psychopaths, and they don't feel embarrassed or guilty. The typical person who tries to provoke gas will be unsurprising since their body language and facial expressions will tell the impression. They can also be convincing liars and manipulators, much as psychopaths, and they don't give their victims any clues as to the actions they're taking. Their aim is to erase the perception of the reality of their targets by telling lies that are true.

The term gaslighting was first used in the stage show Gas Light in the late 1930s. It was an British production which introduced the general public to the concept of gaslighting. What is psychological abuse? It takes the form of providing victims with false information to make them make them doubt their knowledge and memory. It was the Gas Light play finally moved to the U.S. under the name Angel Road. There were two films adapted to the game in the beginning of the 1940s. In 1940, there was an British film titled Gaslight and in 1944, there is an American film titled Gaslight. Both films featured an abuser who is able to manipulate his victim's mental state. The perpetrator has a spouse who makes her wife in to a target through making her feel guilty by lighting her up.

In essence, he is trying to convince his wife and friends that to believe that she's insane. He manipulates the elements of his surroundings, and later asserts his wife's in error in her attempt to recall what the objects were originally. Gaslighting is a reference to an animated show where the husband utilizes gas lamps to search through his home to find hidden treasure. When he does this the gas lights dim across his home. His wife is able to see the dim glowing light and confronts him and denies the incident ever occurred. Psychologists as well as laypeople have used gaslighting since the time of the play and movies were created to explain this type of psychopathic behavior.

The term "gaslighting" refers to the manipulation in which mental abuse is used. The perpetrator also exposes their victims to false information so that they will be viewed more favorably by them. The goal of the abuser is to make their victims be concerned about their own safety and their memory of a particular situation. They will not see the person who is committing the act as doing any wrong by doing this. Gaslighting is often performed by psychopaths, those who suffer from personality disorders that are which is characterised by a lack regret and a rise in aggressive behavior.

These personality traits enable people to manipulate others for psychopaths without feeling embarrassed or guilty. People who are typical and try to put on a show will be unsurprising since their body language and facial expressions will tell an indication of. They can also be effective liars, manipulators and liars like psychopaths, but without providing their victims any clues as to the actions they're taking. Their aim is to eradicate the understanding of the reality of their targets by creating lies that are accurate.

The term gas lighting was first introduced in the stage show Gas Light in the late 1930s. It was an British production that introduced the public to the concept of gas lighting. We discussed what this meant

4

in terms of psychological abuse that consisted of giving victims false information that makes them doubt their own perception and memory. This Gas Light play finally moved to the U.S. under the name Angel Road. Two films were made in adaptation to the game in the beginning of the 1940s. In 1940, there was the British film titled Gaslight while in 1944, there were two films, one of which was an American film titled Gaslight. Both films featured an abuser who manipulates his victim's mental state. The victim can be a man who transforms the wife of his through inducing her to do.

In essence, he is trying to convince her and the rest of the world that to believe that she's insane. He manipulates different elements in his surroundings and then claims the wife's in error in her attempt to remember what they were before. The idea of gaslighting comes from a TV show where the husband makes use of gas lamps to search inside his home for treasures that are hidden. If he does this, the gas lights turn off across your home.

The wife spots the dim light and confronts him and denies the incident ever took place. Psychologists as well as laypeople have used gaslighting since the play and movies were created to depict this type of psychopathic behavior.

Chapter 1: 3 Different Methods of Manipulation

This section we'll discuss ways to set limits in the face of truly manipulative individuals. Through this article, you'll be able to recognize the various ways that people are able to manipulate you , and more importantly, you will remain aware of such techniques and how to deal with these tactics to ensure that your boundaries are not violated. We'll discuss about the most common methods that people can manipulate you, and the ways in which these tactics affect you, and more importantly, what you can do to counter these techniques to counter the tactics and why we attempt to manipulate one another. People who manipulate and those who manipulate pull are two different sides of the same coin They're stuck in a situation whereby they are trying to control other person in some manner to feel secure. They also appreciate the sense that they're contributing to something or feeling that they'll be okay.

Someone who is a manipulative will be trying their best to satisfy people and is trying to earn leftovers of food, recognition or affection. Someone who is manipulative will get the same kind of manipulative or valuable by controlling other people. If they are able to convince you to perform a task for them which you don't want do , or exerts some sort of control over you this means they must be significant and that means you truly care about them. If you truly care to them deeply, you'll perform certain actions to help them. This is the Nutshell on why people play games with one another and the reason they are compelled to do it in the first place. You aren't able to stop the people who are manipulating since it's just an energetic response to two individuals who want to be controlled. You can't create the reality of someone else.

You only have the power to create your own reality but you cannot do anything to prevent people from doing something or being unable to do something. It's possible to try however it's not going to succeed. What you need to do is assert the power you have and alter your personal behavior to ensure that you're no longer susceptible to being controlled and do this by knowing the different methods people use to influence you. You should also anticipate their attempts often enough to be able to recognize how you can respond to them. That's why this article is about. We are going to look at the most effective ways the narcissist manipulates the individual. Some of these tactics may be familiar to you but others might be brand new to you. So If you've got individuals in your life who have been manipulating you, it is possible that you can recognize these actions. The majority of these will be related to shifting your mindset and not focusing on someone else's face or being able to make an amazing comeback at the right time.

Gaslighting

The first is called gas-lighting. When someone is snooping around on you, they are seeking to make you believe that their rules are arbitrary and untrue. When something bothers you and something they've or has been mentioned, they're trying to prove their argument that it is nonsense and no one would ever ever react like that. They also will say that they don't care about anyone other than you, and that you're just too sensitive. Spiritual people aren't in any way immune to this, as there are people who will tell you that if more educated, then it shouldn't bother you. Therefore, the manipulative and gaslighting technique is basically to force you to loosen your limits by convincing you to doubt your boundaries, and then convincing yourself that the boundaries that you set for yourself are ineffective and ineffective, and you ought to drop them.

Your line of sight isn't the responsibility of anyone else Nobody can decide the boundaries you'll have. If you are unhappy with something and you are unhappy,

10

nobody is obliged to explain to you how they are feeling. If you're being slapped in the arm repeatedly over and again when you say to them "please do not striking me in the arms," and the person responds with"I don't think you're punching me in the arm," or "I'm in no way hitting you so hard" it's not their responsibility to determine if the striking bothers you, but it's really your decision. If you are able to create a boundary that is like that be sure to keep in mind that you're fighting for the boundary as well as the right to establish boundaries, not for an actual boundary. Don't let someone claim the boundary you have set isn't large enough to warrant the necessary stand. That kind of thinking is a complete disrespect.

It's a huge offense to step within someone else's boundaries. You should be aware that there's a distinction between directing someone else's behavior when you tell the person how to behave in a certain way, and setting boundaries by telling that person to not behave the way you want them to. Setting boundaries means you will be required to distance yourself from the person or thing if they are causing harm to you. You should now recognize that it'sn't to stop someone ending their life as they'd like to live it and it's not about restricting their freedom from them. It's about making the decision to be a part of the conversation or not engaging with those who are a certain way or don't adhere to your rules.

The setting up of an angry beast

The second method of manipulating is to turn into an angry monster This is where someone is trying to be more angry than you in an attempt to stifle your anger or rage. In other words, you may get off at something, but when you confront the person, that you are angry, he'll get angry and the situation will become so massive that you get yourself back to. You'll be shocked since you had been discussing something small but they have turned it into something huge and you're not ready to endure that kind of tension. In most cases, you'll be fighting to protect your

12

boundaries in order to avoid this scenario or explode.

What they do is to attack you with an emotional reaction which is so overwhelming that it doesn't seem worth the cost for the item you're trying defend. In order to make you retreat and, often you'll never even attempt to defend yourself because you're completely unwilling to confront the beast that is threatening you.

If you're defending the proper boundaries and have set that boundaries, it does not have to be about what that boundary about or take into account whether the person believes it is legitimate or not when you've clearly communicated the boundary. If the other person states that he doesn't accept it , then inform that if he doesn't do this, you're going to break off from him , and quit interacting with him and you'll not be able to access to him any longer. If you've done that and that person crosses the line, you must to defend it or else you won't be able to define any boundaries whatsoever. This means that you be obligated to worry about the consequences of your actions, such as moving against them the other party or letting them out of the bargain. You must do whatever you need to do, as you stated you would do if you were unable to keep the boundaries. However, you need to establish boundaries around things that bother you, and not set boundaries for things that aren't important to you.

Reducing the problem

The next technique to manipulate you is when someone manipulates the subject and then takes the issue off in a different direction to divert you from the main issue to ensure that you don't define or defend the boundary. For example, suppose that your spouse hasn't gotten home from work, and they don't contact you, and you're concerned because they didn't contact you and then they return home and you have no idea exactly where they went. If they do eventually come home and you inform them about the incident and they simply blow it up and say it's not a big deal. Therefore, in this situation it is important to explain to them that this really bothered you and that you want them to contact you. It is also important to you.

As you're having a conversation with them, they may wander off and begin discussing the stress they're experiencing at work and why you're not being a victim. They could talk discussing it, and begin talking about how stressed they're under at work, and you're not going to feel any sympathy for them. If that happens you could end up on the defensive end of the discussion. You could say something like, "I totally understand how stressed you're feeling at work, and I'm sorry, and aren't going to start making excuses to them. When you're done you're not talking about what's troubling you, but you're not talking about what's troubling them.

Then, they've taken over the conversation and shifted into a totally different direction which is why you'll find yourself having to sit them down and apologize to them. You will be feeling like you can't be bothering them with your small matter. These people who employ these tricks are not using them in a deliberate manner. They're not using this deliberately. Therefore, they're not taking over an entire conversation for the purpose of doing so however they're doing it nevertheless. When you realize this happening and you are concerned, stop and walk out of the room.

There's no need for trying to convince yourself back to your original subject. Allow it to go for a time, then put a pin on it, and when the time comes such as the following morning, when things are slightly calmer or in the evening, you could return to the topic again. It is best to bring it up the next day, and should someone try to put it off simply tell them that you're not going to divert the conversation by focusing on something that is important to you. If they aren't willing to take that step, then move on until you can return to the topic. If you have an individual who isn't willing to engage in a conversation with you, you must quit the relationship. However, you must be able to hold this conversation and not let them get in the way of your plans. However, you shouldn't be required to engage in that conversation with those who are angry, especially when you're in a relationship that is toxic. If you're in a relationship that they will always agree with you and you're not sure if they're right, then reconsider the relationship.

Chapter 2: Gaslighting The Vital Narcissistic

You want to feel sympathy for your family members, but they seem to have evaded your thoughts lately. Your friends don't have the least idea of what you're complaining about when you rant about your strained relationship. They believe that your spouse is a perfect holy messenger. Your family is confused about your bizarre behavior. Everyone believes that you've been totally insane. You try to get out of the confusion, but your accomplice is always in the background to tell the world that you're ineffective determined, persistent poor, and insane. Perhaps his family and others are also a firm believer of him. They do not seem to be a fan of the way you look. The appeal of his has influenced everyone else. You are wondering if you're the person at cause of the problem. In all honesty how can anyone else recognize the fact that your partner is responsible for the decline in your emotional wellbeing? Why can't they feel the same way? You aren't feeling like you anymore. You're feeling like an unrecognizable self. You were vibrant and full of life before you encountered the narcissist who is in your life. You love him but you feel that he's taking you down at the same time. You're wondering why your bond isn't as strong, loving and filled with self-improvement. The issue is that it's difficult to tell which of you is crazy. At first you knew that it was him. However lately you're wondering whether your personal sense that you are in a state of calm is diminishing. You are feeling unmotivated, exhausted and exhausted and confused. You are afraid that you could even experience a mental breakdown anytime in the near future. Some people do not comprehend. A majority of people don't have a idea what is happening. If you're experiencing this there's a simple reason. You could be in a relationship or tied to someone who is a person who is a narcissist. Your self-indulgent accomplice could be smothering you and controlling your behavior. He could be alternating between smothering you with praise and then separating his self from the other. By all accounts, a good person to be around every now and then but then you notice that he's negative about you to others. He is able to link you with women or friends to attract your attention and encourage his internal self. Does he chatter you around and around whenever you come into his face about his location when he's in a hurry? Do you discover that you're generally overly excited' and 'excessively weak' when you tell him that you must establish a rapport? Do you feel he is cautious whenever you have to advance the relationship in any way? Do you have a tendency to avoid any activity that is akin to development or obligation? Does he cut you off from family members in order to ensure to have the chance to convince everyone to join his cause? Are you prevented from enjoying any freedom as there is a fear of the chance that you'll be leaving him?

Does his confidence wane to the point that you are imagining that you could think about cheating if you speak with someone else? Are you worried about making sense' of what you is doing, especially if people around you agree with you? In the event that the majority of these are a concern for you, you're an innocent victim of gaslighting.

Gaslighting is a form of psychological abuse in which the perpetrator controls events repeatedly to trick the victim to doubt their personal memories and experiences. Gaslighting is a method of deceitful of abuse. It causes victims to question the very notions they've relied on for throughout their lives, leaving them doubtful about anything. The gaslighting process makes it more likely for the person to be able to accept what their abusers tell them, regardless of their personal involvement in the situation. Gaslighting can be a precursor to different types of violent and physical violence due to the fact that the victim will likely to remain in various other threatening situations too. The phrase "gaslighting" is derived in the 1938 British production "Gas Light,"" in which a husband and wife attempt to force his spouse insane by performing a variety of tricks that force her to question her perceptions and mental stability. "Gas Light" was turned into a motion movie in both 1940 and 1944.The phrase "gaslighting" has been used in conversations since the 1960s to depict attempts to alter the perception of someone's the world. The term has been used to describe such behavior within psychoanalytic texts since the 70s. In a book published in 1980 about child sexual abuse, Florence Rush outlined George Cukor's Gaslight (1944) in the light of the play. She wrote, "even today the word gaslighting is used to describe an attempt to defy another's perception of reality."

Signs of Gaslighting

Gaslighting is a hazard that can be detected with various indicators, such as the ones below

You think you are an entirely different person.

You're more anxious and less self-confident than you were previously.

You are very sensitive.

You are convinced that every move you make is wrong.

You're constantly thinking you're making a mistake whenever you experience a problem.

You often apologize.

There are times when you feel like things are not going as planned however, you are in a position to determine the reason or even why.

There are many questions asked about whether the way you respond to your partner's behavior was appropriate (e.g. you are speculating whether you were uninformed or not affectionate enough).

You always find excuses for your spouse's actions.

You're avoiding providing information to household associates or friends to avoid hostility towards your spouse.

You are feeling isolated from your friends and family.

It is becoming getting harder to decide what to do.

You're depressed and have little or no interest in things that you used to love.

Are You Gaslighted Do You Really Feel Gaslighted?

Find the gaslighter.

Below is a list of Twenty Revealing Secret symptoms:

Gaslighting may not cover all of these knowledge-based as well as emotional state, however when you are a victim of one or more of them, consider giving the subject some thought.

1.You constantly re-think your thoughts.

2. You think, "Am I excessively delicate?" twelve times each day.

3. Sometimes, you feel confused or even crazy when you work.

4. You're always saying sorry to your father, mom, dad or boss, beau.

5. You wonder much of the time if you are an "adequate" sweetheart/spouse/worker/companion/partner.

6. There's no reason to believe that when you have such a large number of clearly beneficial things happening in your life there isn't a greater sense of joy.

7. You purchase clothes to wear, things to furnish your home or for other people with your partner in mind taking into consideration what he may prefer rather than what will make you feel amazing.

8. A lot of times, you justify your partner's behavior to your loved ones.

9. It is easy to deny information from family members which means you don't need to justify or clarify.

10. You know something is completely off-base, but you're unable to not fully articulate the issue to yourself.

11. You try to avoid the snarky comments and then reality takes over.

12. You have difficulty coming to easy choices.

13. It is advisable to reconsider the discussion before bringing up the seemingly innocent subjects of debate.

14. After your partner has returned at home, you review all of your thoughts to imagine what you might have missed that day.

15. You have the feeling that you used to be an altogether different individual-- progressively certain, increasingly carefree, progressively laid back.

16. You begin to address your significant partner through his administrator, so you don't have to divulge to him the things that could cause him to become angry.

17. It's as if you're incapable of doing anything right.

18. Children begin to protect you from the other.

19. People can be angry, especially those who you have a good relationship with before.

20. You are more emotional or sensitive. You feel overwhelmed and overburdened.

The Precisely Myself Show Revealed the Gaslight The Upshot? ?

There was something incredibly popular about these stories and I was constantly aware that, in addition to truth that I was listening to them as an expert, they also reflected experiences that my friends as well as me had. In each case the woman who seemed to be influential was paired with a sweetheart and/or companion , partner or boss that made her beg her to reconsider her perception of reality and left her confused, confused and deeply discouraged. These relationships were more remarkable due to the fact that across different fields women seemed to be so strong and united. However, there was always one truly exceptional person-- adored boss, friend or even a relative-- whose approval she was constantly trying to gain, even though his assessment of her appeared to shift from average to worse. Finally, I had the choice of giving this gruelling form the name of The Gaslight Effect, after the classic film Gaslight. The great 1944 film tells the story of Paula young and apathetic singer (played by Ingrid Bergman) who weds Gregory who is a charming and astonished guy (played by Charles Boyer). In the dark, unbeknownst to Paula her beloved husband attempts to turn her insane in order to control her legacy. He repeatedly informs her she's sick and fragile as well as reworks family matters and then blames her for what she did and, most cleverly of all, he controls the gas so that she can see the lights dim for no reason. In the midst of her husband's evil plan, Paula begins to accept that she's going insane. Incredulous and scared she begins to act like a lunatic, eventually becoming the fragile, confused person that he keeps revealing to her. In a harrowing downward spiral as she begins to question her own self, the more confused and crazy she ends up becoming. She is desperate for her partner to be there for her and to confess that he loves her, but he is not to reveal this and insists that she is insane. Her transition to mental stability and self-assurance is triggered after a police detective tells her that he too is seeing the dimming of the bright light. As Gaslight clarifies the gaslighting process has two parties. Gregory must entice Paula to make him feel better and more in control. However, Paula is additionally anxious to be lured. She has romanticized this strong attractive, handsome man, and is desperate to believe that he will cherish and be supportive of her. When the relationship becomes serious it is difficult for her to criticize the behavior or think differently about him but she'd prefer to keep her romantic image of the ideal husband. The uncertainty about her and her praise of him provides the ideal opportunity to control his behavior. In Gaslight the gaslighter appears following something that is unmistakable. He is determined to make his wife unhappy so that he will be able to take his property. Gaslighters in general aren't such a shrewd, however, the consequences of their behavior could be a bit naughty in reality. From the viewpoint of the gaslighter it's simply trying to protect his own safety.

Gaslighters have such a fragile sense of self-esteem that he's unable to endure the most arduous test of how his perception of things. However, he prefers to reveal the world to himself. That's the way you should view it. Or, make him vulnerable to a tense anxiety. Let's suppose you smile at someone in a social gathering and you are feeling uncomfortable. A person who isn't gaslighting could say, "Better believe it, I'm the envy type," or, "I know you didn't do any wrong thing Dear, but it is crazy to watch you play around with the other guys." The person is willing to think that his plight could result from the circumstances or his own insecurities. No matter if you were engaging in sexual activity, the nongaslighter might possibly conclude that your behaviour that he finds shocking it, isn't intended for him to feel bad even though you may also ask that you end the flirting. The gaslighter does not consider that his personal need, weakness or neurosis might be part of. The gaslighter sticks with his personal explanation: he's feeling terrible because you're flirting. He's not content just realizing that it's possible; he wants for you to accept. In the event that you do not, you'll be able to be greeted with long-lasting periods of rage, anger and hurt feelings, or what he believes to be sensible analysis. ("I don't even have the slightest idea of why you don't realize the extent to which you're hurting me. Do my words make any difference to you in any way?") It takes two to dance and gaslighting could occur only in the event of a gaslightee who is willing or someone who is awed by the gaslighter but desperately needs his support. If you're not averse to gaslighting, you might just chuckle and dismiss the argument when your dream romantic partner accuses you of things. If you're not sure, think of that you cannot accept that the person you love so much sees you in an unflattering perspective. Then you could be tempted to fight, trying to convince him to change his view. Like the person who is gaslighted is in a rush to persuade his love to apologize, so too is the person who is being gaslighted desperate to get his approval. She could end up being prepared to do whatever it takes to improve the relationship with her lover, even if it means letting him have a negative, fundamental view of her.

Chapter 3: Gaslighting The Narcissist's Most Favorite Method Of Manipulation

The person who is manipulative at heart. Of all the tools that the can make use of to manipulate you according to their wishes their most popular tool is gaslighting. Gaslighting is a devious manipulative technique where the narcissist makes you wonder if they're losing their mind. The narcissist instills doubt and doubt in your mind to serve the sole purpose of getting control over you.

You are aware of yourself. You are aware of your thoughts, opinions and convictions. You know precisely what you believe in, and what you don'tor at least, you did. But, since the narcissist entered your life, you've been experiencing a lot of confusion and uncertainty about everything. It's difficult to remember things in the right way now. You're never certain about your decisions. You're constantly in a state of panic in a state of doubt, wondering if it's possible to be sure of your own thoughts. You start to think that you're being crazy, but it's not true. It's because the Narcissist has successfully slapped you.

The Roots of "Gaslighting"

The phrase "gaslighting" was accepted as a lingo because of the 1944 film named "Gaslight." This isn't to say that gaslighting or narcissists didn't exist. existed before the film, however. In the film the man brainwashes his wife into believing she has lost her mind. When he turned on the gas light in the above-ground apartment the house, his wife would notice that the lights at their home would dim. But, he would constantly convince her that she had only thought of things.

One of the most painful aspects when you are a victim gazlighting is the fact that it could result in Stockholm Syndrome where the victim starts to look at the narcissist for guidance on what to think and what to be feeling, as well as what the reality. Even you can become apathetic to the narcissist because you begin to have negative thoughts as "How extremely frustrating it will be for them to endure my unreliable memories!"

If you've been the sufferer of gaslighting then you could not be able to recognize the person who is causing the harm for what they truly are. This isn't because you're dumb but more likely the narcissist will take you by surprise and captivate your head. They're so attractive that you feel like a rotten person for a long time, constantly second-guess or questioning them. They make that charm the surface that you cease being a believer in your own intuition and begin believing in them. It's not obvious that you've been taken into a dangerous and violent relationship.

Let's take a take a look at some ways that the narcissist can mess with your gas lamps and other electrical equipment without even realizing it.

Classic Gaslighting Techniques and their effects

Reframing. This is when the gaslighter alters or alters the events to make it sound like they were the hero or the victim of the whole incident and you're the culprit. You begin to wonder if you're mistaken about what believed they intended to do. They often try to frame the situation with a lack of empathy, which makes you feel more insanity and uncertainty that you feel. If, for instance, the victim slaps you and you are certain that they intended to hurt you then they could respond, "Oh come on, I didn't strike you this in the way! It was just a moment or fun fighting. Don't make a big fuss about this."

The subject of switching. The gaslighter who is narcissistic will decide to switch topics instead of addressing the question they're asking, or the argument you're trying to make. They'll usually reply, "No, you imagine the same thing as you did with that other idea. Did your friend make you think of the same silly thoughts?"

Then they've made it about a person they dislike instead of focussing on the problem in question.

The act of downplaying. The gaslighter makes your thoughts and feelings appear unimportant to the point that you begin to wonder why you're always so sensitive over things. The more they make you feel unimportant the more power they'll hold over you.

Denial. I once heard an exchange between two teenagers in a mall. One of them was having problems in the house and discussing it with the other. When her mother discovered the story that she was in trouble, she did the one option she knew she could do to avoid trouble. In her own words, she stated, "Deny, deny, deny until you're dead." It seemed like a mantra way she said it and I've struggled to take it out of my mind since.

The gaslighting strategy used by the narcissist. You can tell that they were saying something or doing something and you witnessed to it through your eyes and hearing. Yet, they don't admit the fact that they were there. Sometimes, it's because they didn't know you were watching them. They realize that you watched them do the things they did. Yet, they'll openly refuse to admit that they did. This denial can confuse you. It's normal to ask whether your mind is working in the right way, since normal people would not be tempted to fake story when they're aware they've been victimized by it.

This isn't the case with the gaslighter. They're no problem going in the direction of insisting that you prove the validity of what you're saying. This is an excellent instance of gaslighting because in certain circumstances the only thing you have is your memories of what happened. In this way, you might be tempted to ask yourself whether they're correct and you're incorrect. Perhaps you're the one who is crazy You think.

Outright Lies. It's not just that the narcissist utters outright lies that will leave you stunned, but it's the ease in their lies that are shocking. They're extremely at ease with their lies. They promote "crazy-making," presented so easily that you think you're somewhat crazy for not being a believer.

Killing you softly. Narcissists have the goal of turning you appear to be a shell of the person you really are. You might not realize the more they smear you and the more you give to them and turn into an individual you can't identify anymore. They take your life - so gently - and slowly, erases the person you truly are, leave behind an image can play with as they want.

Utilizing your treasures against You. Do you enjoy your job? Your kids? Your pet? The abuser isn't afraid of using anything you hold dear and dear to use in their gaslighting tactics. They're adept at making people believe that you are not worthy of the kind things or people that you have in your life. You are left wondering the reason you're blessed If they've done the job correctly it wi l be a sabotage to your relationships and achievements that you value.

Love Bombing. The reason why gaslighting works so effectively as a manipulative method is because the narcissist manipulates you to be ok with abuse using methods like carrots and sticks. If they feel that they've spread the lies, denial, or inexcusable punishment and will then follow it with a plethora of flattery and love. An excellent example of this is the man that beats up his spouse to purchase diamonds for her, or a woman who cuts down her husband in order to cook him his most loved meal or lavishly entertain his acquaintances in the hope that she has taken him too far and may end up losing the man. Narcissists will make use of charm and affection to lure you back to get more abuse. The problem is that you become used to being constantly miserable and victimized. If they're adoring and pleasing you, you're thinking that to yourself "Well it's not as terrible than I imagined. I'm not sure why I was so angry. I'm still here."

Are You Being Gaslighted?

It isn't easy to know if this really is true, on because of the extent to which the perpetrator may have played with your mental health in the present. I've put together the following list of questions that you should consider asking yourself to ensure you can identify whether you're the victim of gaslighting.

1. Do you frequently consider, "Why am I so sensitive?" throughout the day?

2. Are you constantly making excuses?

3. Do you think you're somewhat crazy or are you constantly confused in your relationship with the person you're with?

4. Do you feel that you're constantly experiencing a feeling that something isn't right with your relationships, even though you're unable to pinpoint the cause on it?

5. Are you constantly wondering what's wrong with you? as you could be?

6. Are you struggling to even make the most basic of choices?

7. Are you finding yourself finding excuses after excuse to justify the way your spouse behaves towards you?

8. Do you feel like you're always feeling that you'll never be able to meet the standards of your spouse?

If you're able to answer yes to these questions and you're not suffering from low self-esteem, depression or anxiety-related disorders, you're probably being criticized by this individual or by the people that cause you to feel like this in your life. Examine your interactions with people you live with and observe the people whom you are constantly experiencing these things. If you're only ever feeling the same way with one individual or group of people then it's likely you're a gaslight victim.

Chapter 4: Self-Care after Gaslighting

Self-care is an edgy word in the mass media. But don't believe that self-care is just the latest trend. Self-care is a fundamental part of any lifelong habit even if the person isn't recovering from being gaslighted. Self-care is the act of giving yourself the opportunity to feel worthy of your time and attention, and to deliberately provide yourself with attention and time. It's not the same thing as being selfish or self-indulgent. Self-care should be about renewal the body, healing and releasing anything that is hindering you from becoming satisfied and happy. This chapter will help not only in gaslighting your recovering, but also by understanding how to make yourself feel important. Your reality is constantly being altered by the world around you, and this will give you a say in the way you want your reality to appear.

Self-Care Recovery

The self-care techniques described within this section is designed to overcome the psychological and emotional abuse of gaslighting. Of course, these strategies could be used again and redirected for different purposes but the main goal is to help you restore your emotional balance and teach yourself the security to restore your life.

Each chapter is identified by the purpose of each section. There are instances when you need physical or emotional renewal or physical renewal, etc. That's the reason this chapter is divided in this manner. These are not steps in a sequential order but are intended to be easy-to-use. You're supposed to have control over your life right now, and making self-care your own responsibility is an excellent method of establishing control over yourself and eliminate the influence of your abuser.

The first step is to stop and examine your emotions. Most likely, you're experiencing sadness, anxiety or simply uncomfortable.

Find out how your feelings manifest. Are they causing you to go through a rough emotional rollercoaster? Do you feel the tension in your shoulders and causing you to get a headache? Are you feeling lost and confused, like you are unable to keep track of everything? Are you overwhelmed by the sounds and feelings that overwhelm you at close of the day? Utilize these questions to determine which type of self-care can best address what you want. Go through the list of suggestions and choose one that is appealing to you. Choose one, then pick five, then choose one, pick five, then choose all. You are at ease mixing and matching in case you are experiencing different kinds of stress. It could be beneficial to keep a journal where you write down the things you did every day and how they affected your mood. It is possible to use a basic scale of a smiley face or frowny smile or something more complex such as a rating system. Whatever you decide to use ensure that you're taking note of it at the very the very least, to ensure that you will know which self-care methods are most beneficial for you. It is not a good idea to engage in self-care that's not improving you to improve your "self."

Self-Care Techniques categorized by category

1. Self-care for the emotional

If you're constantly getting caught up in a storm of emotions, then this might be the ideal type of self-care option for you. Your emotions are created to shift frequently, however you shouldn't feel as if your life is uncertain and difficult to comprehend. It's time to step off the rollercoaster and experience some stability.

*Make a list with a few feeling words that you keep handy to refer to. This may sound like a joke and yet, often the reason reasons we can't communicate our emotions is that we don't have a word for these feelings. Make emotion more understandable by giving it the name. Don't settle for "angry" even if you happen to be "infuriated." When you are able to identify your opponent you will find it much easier to defeat it. It is possible to keep these lists in a specific location or even add it to any journal you are keeping. You can refer to it frequently and be sure to research definitions whenever you want to. Your feelings are yours to control. It's time to take control of them once more, rather than the abuser dictating what you feel.

"Feeling emotions" means to express emotions. If you are able to identify the emotion, let it take shape in the time the sensations you experience. If you're feeling grieving, you can cry. If you're angry then hit the pillow to the maximum force you can at least as many times that you are able to. If you're feeling smiling, allow yourself to smile as much that you are able to. It is likely that you've held in all the emotions that are true because you were worried about the way your abuser might react. This is the perfect moment to let it go however it comes. It's as messy or messy as you need it to be, since you're at liberty right now.

Record what you feel and doing. It's been said several times before and keeping a record of your experience is an effective tool for many reasons. The most important reason is that it can help you recognize patterns within your own life. It is simple to forget and forgive if you don't realize how often you need to forgive. You might be ignoring the fact that you're suffering more frequently than you're being treated. It is the same about self-care. If you discover that you're not engaged in self-care regularly, think about the reason why. There's an emotional reason that is at the root and addressing this is another type of self-care that is emotional.

2. Physical Self-Care

If you feel that your body is constantly tangled into knots, then it could be the physical manifestations of the abuse you've endured. The anxiety and stress associated with gaslighting typically affect your physical health, in the forms of insomnia and sudden weight loss or gain, and severe tension in joints and muscles. These exercises are designed to loosen knots and allow your body to relax to let your mind relax.

*If you're feeling too worked up, take the time to rest. Don't be afraid of this suggestion. A short, but long nap can have a significant impact on your body's feeling of wellbeing. To avoid disrupting a regular routine of sleep, schedule nap times that last from 20 to 30 minutes. You should ensure that you are napping in a location which is secure and lets your body rest fully. Make a plan for your nap time so that you are looking at it with anticipation and be responsible for providing the much-needed relaxation.

If your muscles are always tight, you should try yoga and/or stretching. It sounds more like an exercise to warm up than a real workout on its own However it is an excellent method to relax and stimulate your body to go into a deep and relaxing sleep. It's also a great method to get up if you've were having trouble getting to sleep. Stretching your muscles can help you relax and move ahead quicker. Yoga is similar to yoga in that manner, and may be beneficial in creating positive social interaction when you attend an exercise class.

If you're not happy with the way that abuse has affected the way you feel or how your energy levels have changed Find an exercise that helps you feel better about your body and the things it is able to accomplish. It's not the same for all. It is possible to choose one type of exercise, or several. It may be a high-impact or low impact routine. If you can get your body moving regularly it will improve both your physical and mental health at the same time. Don't be afraid to take on things outside the norm. If your idea of exercising is to make an unplanned time to dance in the living room you should do it. This is a natural expression happiness, and it can make your body feel satisfied. If your body is content and content, it becomes easy for your mind to follow.

3. Mental Self-Care

It is possible that emotional self-care and mental self-care are similar However, the concept of mental self-care revolves around systematic and methodical thinking processes. That's why self-care for the mind is an crucial forms of self-care, as an orderly mind is more adept at managing stress. It is possible that you are not capable of controlling your emotions however, having a mental state capable of helping you identify the problem and deal with it head-on is hugely beneficial.

Don't undervalue the power of the power of a list. Lists come in a variety of types and formats, however it is not difficult to feel the feeling of satisfaction when you cross the items off of an agenda. They can be used to do with something simple or something more complex. It is possible to create an annual grocery list to help you eat healthier. You could also create an outline of your emotional goals for the week. For instance, writing every night, or engaging with self-care 3 times a week.

Write these lists down by writing them down on paper, using your smartphone, using an app, or inside an organizer. The location doesn't matter. The mental process of organising what you want to achieve is what is important and will help you to be more confident.

It's possible that you don't know that you are taking care of yourself today. Reading is an excellent method of self-care as it allows you to explore and discover new things. It also allows you to take a journey into a different world or an entirely new subject which allows you to unwind from worrying about the current. It also lets you explore a part of the globe without being influenced from the person who is your abusive partner. They are no longer able to control the content you consume as an avid reader. The need to take a break from the mind is essential and reading a good book is an excellent option to get it done.

Try something new or work on the puzzle of your choice. This is an excellent activity for someone who has been gaslighted because of the belief that you cannot control your reality. If you're able to be a new person or solve a problem that was difficult to solve it is not simply taking control of your life, but you are doing something that you've not done before. It is a good opportunity to increase confidence in yourself and remind yourself that you're capable of growing as an individual.

4. Sensory Self-Care

This one may be confusing since you've not considered your sensory requirements. But, the sensory stimulation we experience every day could overburden our nervous system and lead to anxiety and stress. Gaslighting can make you feel as if you're living in a state of confusion. Inviting yourself back into the natural world and ensconce your body in concrete soothing feelings is the ideal way to let the fog go and find your way out.

Take a walk in a serene area that is peaceful. It's individual for everyone however if you'd prefer more specific guidelines choose a spot which is peaceful and has a low amount of walking traffic, has lots of plants growing and perhaps an audio you enjoy. Some sounds you might like include running water , or the sound of leaves swaying among the tree. It is possible that you enjoy the sounds of the birds so try seeking for an area with a bird sanctuary. Perhaps you love the feeling of sand, so check whether you can locate an area of sand or beach in which you can walk. This might require several trials and errors but before you are done, you'll find some natural areas that feel like a secure harbour when you are in need of some peace. It's likely that nature isn't the place you prefer to be, so you should think about the same factors. You should ensure that it is peaceful, quiet, and offers soothing music. It could be a place like the library, where conversations and loud noises are not an issue.

There's a lot of research that demonstrates the effectiveness of music. Music is an amazing source to take your mind to many different places. Pick any music that you enjoy however, you must make it that is most appropriate for your mood. This is a great method for people who have trouble expressing their emotions in public. People are often triggered by music. Allow the music to allow you to cry, smile, laugh Relax, smile, or cry. Music can help you achieve emotional release and ease some of the stress of being vulnerable emotionally.

Breathing can be a powerful weapon against anxiety and stress. It's easy, cheap and highly effective. It is not necessary to have any manual or guidance before you try a breathing exercise. All you need to do is breathe slowly and in a deep way. It is helpful to keep a count while you breathe in and out , but only to ensure your breath is controlled and not too rapid. An easy way to do this without having to think about something similar to an alarm clock is to make use of your fingers. Breathe in while you raise each finger and out when you put every finger back down. Another method is to use a breathing rollercoaster. This will give you the added sensational benefit of touch. One hand extends the pointer of your finger. Utilizing the other hand, expand all of your fingers. Take your pointer finger and begin at the outer edge of your thumb. While you trace the sides of your thumb take a deep breath. When you trace down the opposite hand, exhale until you get to the bottom. Repeat this process as you trace down and up every finger you hold until you get to the top.

Chapter 5: Understanding Gaslighting

"Gaslighting" can be interpreted as a symbolic word which refers to emotional abuse with a deceitful manner. Perhaps the victimizer will present false facts to their victims so that they could better understand them. The aim of the victimizer is cause their victims to doubt their own health and recall about a specific circumstance. We aren't looking at the person who died as having been wrong in any manner.

Gaslighting is usually committed to insane people who suffer from uncharacteristic issues that are distinguished by their lack of compassion towards others and a more aggressive behaviour. These traits of character can lead to the abuse of others by people who are deranged and without feeling embarrassed or regretful about the act. People who are accustomed to looking for a gas light will likely be uneasy about it because they will be able to resign themselves to their non-verbal communication as well as exterior appearances. But they could be powerful and liars, as well as controllers, as insane individuals, not ever revealing what they're doing to their victims. Their goal is to undermine the understanding of truth through their motives, causing falsehoods to appear legitimate.

"Gaslighting" began to be used through the stage show "Gas Light" in the final quarter during the late 1930s. It was an British play that brought gaslighting to the general population. We looked at how it suggested mental abuse by providing victims with fake information so that they could doubt their own comprehension and memory.

The Gas Light play moved to the United States under the name Angel Road. Two film adaptations of the play occurred during the 1940s midway through the decade. In 1940 there was an British film called "Gaslight," and in 1944, there was an American film was released called "Gaslight." Both motion films featured an aggressor who used a meticulous mental control of his victim.

The victim is the spouse who, by gaslighting her to make a victim of his spouse. He tries to convince her and other people that she's insane. He accomplishes this by controlling the various components, then insisting that his wife isn't real when she tries to recall what the components functioned.

The phrase "gaslighting" is derived from an episode in the tale in which the spouse uses gas lamps to search his upper-level room in search of hidden treasure. If they do this the gas lights continue appearing dim across the the room. His wife is aware of the lights dimming and confronts her spouse over it, but he denies ever having done it. Both lay and professional therapists are using gaslighting since the films and plays were released to depict the kind of psychotic behavior that is common to.

Gaslighting techniques

The person who employs this technique is usually person who is confided in face-to-face. It can happen within the home or among friends but the greatest interest is with the couple in which this method has compensated for time lost.

This kind of abuse begins by creating uncertainty in the victim and closings, causing the person to lose the notion of the truth.

In some situations, the victim isolates themselves from the rest of the world, believing that they are free to confide in the person who is enticing them because they seem to be the only one who sees the problem before them. It is a lot more difficult to get out of that enigma.

A few indicators that suggest we might be victims of gaslighting can be seen in the following:

1. You doubt your memory, what you've said or done

The controller begins with a falsehood which could be perceived as real-world scenario. This means they could create a false story about an incident that actually been a fact and force the victim to acknowledge that they missed.

Imagine, for instance you inquire with your companion where the money leftover from the purchase of the month is, and they reveal to you that you did it all on your own, that they can't recall if it was on a Tuesday or Wednesday, however , you took the cash at the moment to purchase your pet.

You think that you made a purchase with credit card because it was a lot of cash, however, this causes you to lose your mind even though you aren't denying it at all.

2. You are left doubting your beliefs about the reality

Imagine you're trying to let them know the fact that something they've spoken or done has irritated you.

For example: "I didn't care for the way you replied to the young lady who revealed our the letter. It seems like there is nothing that can satisfy you. "

A person who is using the gaslighting technique will typically respond to expressions of the following kind:

"You think about it, and I'm the villain."

"You always apply things to your own field."

"You alter reality at your desire, but you aren't aware of the extent of the harm.

You do to me when you make those statements to me that you say to me, and the worst part is you actually believe it , and I think that I am guilty."

3. Unusual behavior of the victim. Causes unusual behavior in the

If the person has created the doubt about the victim's personal judgement, the casualty is able to perform actions that weren't routine before and causes them into the circle of the manipulative person.

One of these practices may be related to:

Refuting your partner's actions

Accepting as fact what the manipulative individual tells you instead of retaining your own view of what actually happened

Making mental checks on the behavior of a person

Checking out the mobile phone of your partner

Refusing to doubt the other person

Asking your friends and acquaintances whether they've seen you recently

Doubting your ability to complete tasks normally done or doubting your abilities to make decisions on your own.

Chapter 6: Narcissist Sociopath, and Psycopath

In order to understand the meaning behind gaslighting It is equally important to become acquainted with these three terms. It helps us to understand the distinction between gaslighting and these terms.

NARCISSIST

Narcissistic personality disorders are identified most often in males; However, women can also be being diagnosed as having the condition. The symptoms include an over-the-top desire to be loved, an indifference to other people's feelings as well as an inability to take any criticism, and a feeling of entitlement. The condition must be evaluated by a qualified professional. The treatment involves talking therapy that assists the patient in navigating their lives with the diagnosis.

Narcissistic personality disorders can create problems in a variety of areas of our lives, such as relationships and work, as well as school or financial matters. People suffering from narcissistic personality disorder might be frustrated and discontent when they are not receiving the recognition they think they deserve. Some may feel that their relationships are not fulfilling as well as others might not like them because of the sensation of being on eggshells.

Signs and symptoms

* Have a false perception of self-importance

* Feel an underlying sense of entitlement and need to be rewarded with constant and unending admiration

* Wish to be seen as superior, even if you haven't achieved anything which justify it.

* Overstate accomplishments and capabilities.

You can be enthralled by fantasies about power, success as well as beauty, brightness or even the perfect mate

* Recognize that they are the best and be connected to similarly extraordinary people

Monopolize discussions and criticize or mock people they consider to be substandard

* Plan for unique rewards and unquestioningly adherence to their needs

* Exploit other people to get what they want

* Experience an inability or resistance to recognize the basic needs and needs of other people

* Be jealous of others and acknowledge that everyone envy them too.

* Behaving in an egocentric or arrogant manner or appearing to be arrogant or pretentious.

* Insist on having the top of everything, for instance, the most luxurious car or office

SOCIOPATH

Sociopath is a term used to describe someone who suffers from the disorder of antisocial personalities (ASPD). The people with ASPD struggle to comprehend other peoples their feelings. They are often prone to break the rules or make decisions impulsively and not feel guilty about the harm they do. Individuals who suffer from ASPD can also play "mind game" to control their friends and family members, colleagues and even strangers. They can be seen as charismatic or charming to some.

Signs and symptoms

* Does not consider any social standards or the laws. They frequently infringe on laws or over-ride the social boundaries.

* Tampers with others and lies using fake names or characters and makes use of others to gain personal attention.

* Does not have any plans for the future. They are also frequently impulsive without taking into account the consequences.

* Displays aggression or irritable behavior. They frequently get into arguments or physically harm other people.

* Never thinks about their own safety or the security of others.

* Can't catch up on professional or personal obligations. This may include being late for work or not paying the bills according to the schedule.

* Doesn't feel guilt or regret over the harm or abuse done to others.

PSYCOPATH

Some psychology terms create confusion, such as the term psychopath. Although it is commonly used to refer to those suffering from mental disorder, it's unofficially diagnosed. The actual definition of psychopath in psychiatry would be the antisocial personality disorder (ASPD). ASPD refers to a person who displays ways of manipulating and causing harm towards other people. "Most people think that it refers to people who are reserved or a loner who keeps the quiet, etc. But, that's not the case with ASPD. "When we refer to someone as antisocial in ASPD is a person who is in violation of society's rules, and other behavior which are more normal."

Signs and symptoms

* socially unresponsible behavior

* not recognizing or abusing the rights of other individuals

* inability to differentiate between the difference between good and evil

* issue with expressing sorrow or sympathy

* the tendency to lie often

• manipulating, harming and causing other people

* reiterating issues with the law

General disregard for security and obligation

SUCH PERSONS MAKE USE GASLIGHTING

Many people are using gaslighting. Below are the roles for gaslighting users who might use it to harm you:

* Cultist

* Dictators

* Boss

* Husband

* Wife

* Parents

* Girlfriend

* Boyfriend
* Narcissist
* Sociopath
* Psychopath

There is a possibility of being gaslighted by many people, it is crucial is to understand whether you've being gaslighted and how you can react . The gaslighter employs a variety of methods and techniques to gain access to your brain.

It's difficult to spot this type of abuse as aside from being a fraud, the person who is gaslighting can also be extremely charming. In the beginning, you might feel uncomfortable that you're thinking you know the truth because of their smiles and lovebombing. The person who is abusing you uses techniques to disprove your suspicions and you soon stop listening to the instincts of your heart.

If it wasn't right the first time you try it, then it's always incorrect, you believe.

This kind of confusion is exactly what the victim is looking for. So you may not even realize that you're in a abusive relationship.

We're done, we've covered all of the above. We'll talk about the way gaslighters work.

The way your narcissist makes use of gaslighting

It's easy to recognize that gaslighting can be dangerous since it allows narcissists gain control over the mind of their partners. Each time someone is narcissistic and gaslights over an insignificant issue seems to be so trivial. What is the point of forcing a scene or break up over whether someone stated that they had a chicken or pork dish during dinner? or if they left home around seven or nine?

The situation becomes increasingly serious once couples begin to make excuses for their the other partners about their relationships with others or ex-partners. But even in this case the retributions they inflict on those who doubt their claims become distractions that take over the conversation.

In time, the accumulation of hundreds or even dozens of instances of gaslighting that occur over a time period of time or even years alters the way a person's brain functions. This also forces the person to be able to see the other person's view of reality by an arrangement of punishment and rewards. Narcissists use this method whenever they face challenges in their control.1 Narcissists first choose to deny the issue, and when confronted by evidence, they will deflect and distract. Whatever method they employ to do it, be it through charm, anger or stonewalling, blame shifting or any other strategy the goal is always to controlling the situation. In a way, by forcing the other person to accept the truth that the narcissist is laying out at any time they maintain the upper hand.

Even when the spouse defends themselves and claims that the narcissist has been lying, the narcissist is able to maintain control by acquiring narcissistic supplies-because the narcissist is not willing to admit that they were wrong.

Narcissists are too indoctrinated to tell the truth. As you observe from the narcissist's signs above they benefit far more to lie than it does anyone else. In any situation they've got nothing in the way of trying to convince others to accept a new view of reality, regardless of whether we accept it or confront them. If you're with a psychopath and you accept that they'll attempt to sway you is part of the way they live their lives.

What do your parents use of gaslighting

Parents' s nagging can go on all the to adulthood, but it could have harmed you in your early years. Children have to be able to trust their own abilities, and if they are taught that what they perceive, hear or feel doesn't really exist and isn't real, it can trigger an entire life of self-doubt. They are unable to think on their own or at the very least, don't allow themselves to practice that capability. That's not good.

* They ignore your unhappy feelings.

It's one thing to try and solve a problem, but it's quite it is a different thing to say that there's nothing wrong at all. Parents are guilty of this when they instruct their children particularly boys not to be emotional. There's there is no "should" nor "shouldn't" in the context of emotions. Individuals can experience whatever they want to feel, and telling them that they're not allowed to invalidate the reasons behind why they're feeling negative.

* They want you to manage your emotions and conceal your actions

Parents are often able to give tips such as "nobody will cause you to feel inadequate or demeaning without your permission" (or more broadly, "nobody can make you feel any way") as well as "you have control over your behavior." It's not the case. We're not machines which can turn our feelings off and on. If we could regulate our emotions we'd be able to choose what we feel about our own preferences, not what's most convenient for other people.

If someone has hurt you, the proper step to take is to accept their apology. Even if they weren't intending to cause harm, the main matter is the act they committed rather than what they wanted to take action. If you claim that someone hurt you, but they claim they weren't responsible, it's similar to telling you how you feel. A parent who is supportive wants to make their child feel better, not argue about whether or not they should feel hurt in the first place.

* They are fond of talking about the wildest dreams you have.

Parents can call children imaginative when they point out things that appear to be real or even things in which the perception is subjective such as spiritual experiences. Saying that something is the product of your imagination is basically what it is. It's called gaslighting. This makes people think that they're not sure what's real and what's not.

They appear to think that your ideas are absurd

If there's a power dynamics between two individuals, which usually is the case in relationships that have large age gap, it's normal for the person with the highest status to misinterpret disagreement as ignorance. If their children aren't with them, their parents might believe they should teach them or that they're being rebellious or ignorant. However, we all have the right to opinions regardless of age. The same thing happens when someone tells you that their comment was an absurd joke and you're exaggerating. This is a frequent type of gaslighting that occurs in intimate relationships.

* They say they're right and you're not with no proof

If someone thinks they're older and wiser than others is able to dismiss great thoughts on anything from direction to the political scene. However, this doesn't mean that if someone corrects your words and you're slammed. If you're prone to turning around to be correct after they discredit your ideas and suggestions, they're disproving your original beliefs.

* They will tell you what you don't like about them.

Parents often tell their children "What is it that you mean when you say you do not like beef? I had steak last week" or "our family is a beach lover." The way you perceive and taste is natural and subjective, therefore no one else is able to dictate that you know what your tastes and preferences are unless they're domineering and preposterous. If they do take away the power to provide people with the right information to be able to treat you with respect.

Psychopaths use gaslighting

Gaslighting is a natural trait for psychopaths, and is their standard method of communication. However, that doesn't mean that someone who is naturally gaslighting is a psychopath.

Gaslighting may be easy for you or it is perhaps not. If it's not the case, then you need to work to make it happen.

A real communicator is not going to be comfortable in a normal environment that is populated by gaslighters, and the reverse is true.

We default to our usual way of communicating whenever we don't have the requirement to adapt to the various methods of communication of others.

Gaslighting can turn people who are particularly lacking of empathy and compassion into gang of fucking idiots who blame others for their troubles, constantly think of themselves as victims, and believe that anyone who is having fun is a bully whom they are obligated to protect all of humanity from.

How your Sociopath utilizes gaslighting

Sociopaths are known to constantly violate social norms violate laws, and abuse others. However, they typically are convincing liars and, at times, attractive ones who constantly deflect responsibility

The sociopath will continue to bombard you with details. It is possible that you want to leave and feel uncomfortable, but the sociopath isn't concerned it will intrude into your privacy and get close to you, and not allowing the space to breathe. It'll feel like you're being 'emotionally squeezed out' due to the fact that you're!

The psychopath will go one step further and will try to get you to feel sympathy and play the victim and give you a tale designed for you to feel bad for him.

Now you're upset that you've been deceived again, and you react in anger at the lies. To distract you from this then, the psychopath will criticize you for not being concerned about them or the problem they're playing victim to. Naturally, they would not want to hear about their tale. The narrative they're feeding youis fabricated and lies, they just are telling this to youto divert you from the actual truth, and to conceal what they've been doing in deceitful ways.

Your boss works employs gaslighting

Everyone has dealt with an unsatisfactory or dismal boss throughout their professional career. It doesn't matter if it's the boss who has a tendency to share too much, the boss with no working/life balance, or boss who is in charge, poor bosses are a source of grievances over happy hours and are the most significant reason for employee turnover in organizations across the country.

Your boss, who is annoying, isn't there to greet you, or acknowledge your work or doesn't take your feedback. In addition, they may give you a few compliments or praise that are unnatural or perhaps uncharacteristically generous. If they create an environment where direct reports are competing with colleagues for praise or opportunities to earn confidence, they create an unequal power dynamics, as well as a lack of trust within the group.

When your manager is able to make your demands or your experience seem irrelevant to their own or to the overall organization when you voice your concerns , and the boss tells you that you're emotional, or making a thing out from nothing or you ought to just follow the rules, the boss may be minimizing your position within the organization. They're also putting your perception of reality by asking you to consider the way you respond to these behavior is appropriate without taking time to consider theirs.

* If you attempt to upset the balance of power by bringing up any issues within your workplace to a snarky boss, you could also be subject to punitive or judgmental punishment , like the boss who is sabotaging your work.

People who are vulnerable to
GASLIGHTING

EMPATHS

Empaths are people who is extremely in tune with the energies of other people. Empaths are also known as energy sponges due to the fact that they absorb emotional hurt surrounding them. In turn empaths are very selfless and strive to improve the lives of everyone around them.

In the case of gaslighting, empaths can be easy targets since they are often unable to separate them from their perpetrators. That is, although empaths are highly sensitive and perceptive empaths tend to lack personal boundaries and are often unable to be able to say "no."

The most common signs of empaths include:

* Moodiness

* Extremely imaginative

* Kind and compassionate nature

* The capacity to take in other's feelings or physical sensations as if an absorbing sponge

* Proficient intuition or the ability to see clearly

* Chaotic or changing emotions

* Sensitiveness intense

* Chronic fatigue + digestive issues

* Attracted to professions that heal.

* Inability to be able to watch violent films

* Anxiety tendencies and addiction

* A tendency to draw injured people

Others who are prone to gaslighting include:

* Mentally weak individuals

* Individual who easily defeats

* People can easily manipulate

* The list goes on and on.

Three ways GASLIGHTER'S ATTACKS THREE WAYS GASLIGHTER'S ATTACK

1.) They sabotage you, usually subliminally.

Gaslighters do operate on subtlety. They mess up your brain in a manner that's frustrating and confusing, in a manner that's not always acknowledged as manipulative. (At least initially). They usually accomplish this by making subtle remarks such as, "You must be imagining that. Did you have a bad night's sleep the night before?" A comment of such a kind can make the victim feel valued rather than being controlled.

2.) They evade arguments and counterpoints.

Another tactic used by gaslighters is deflection. If their victim is brave enough to have the confidence to speak up or disagree with the way they're speaking the gaslighter can dismiss them with a casual grin: "Oh, you're just being too emotional." "You're not feeling unsecure because of your affair." "You're tired from work." exhausted from your job." This tactic causes the victim to feel a bit crazy. The rebuttals that they offer are only going to hurt them as the gaslighter keeps building their argument.

3.) They cause you to doubt everything you believe to be truthful.

The definition of gaslighting is manipulating an individual to the point that they are unsure of their reality. Gaslighters can do this on small medium and large scales. For instance, a gaslighting lover might tell his partner, "There's no way you're exhausted, you've had plenty of rest." It's thought of as an example of a smaller scale. An example of a larger scale could, however, involve contradictions to the obvious; a gaslighting mother may say to her son that he's being punished because he didn't clean the kitchen. Although it is clear that he was the kitchen being cleaned but she'll try to convince him that he did not do this kind of thing.

Chapter 7: What are the Symptoms of Gaslighting

What are some signs of gaslighting that you might observe or feel, or know that you must be aware about? In this article, we'll discuss the signs of gaslighting you must be cautious about.

Blatant Lies

This is one thing you must be aware of. It is a fact that the person who is blaming you is prone to telling. In the end, they are aware they are lying. Why are they so obvious but? It's because they're setting the standard for how they'll be working. For instance, if you begin to hear falsehoods from them, perhaps you'll begin to believe them. You'll begin to question whether what they claim is factual. You're sure it's not true however, whenever you attempt to disprove it you will be told to completely ignore your argument or blame the situation onto you.

The most often is also denial. They'll deny all that's been completed until the day the day they pass away, regardless though they know you have evidence. They often act as if they'd do something and then they'll perform the act, and then when you find them, they will completely refuse to admit the act. Even if they have evidence they'll claim that you're creating it, you're insane, and they're lying.

Do you really believe that you are lying?

Nope. However, they will battle with you until they give up. Their aim in mind is to ensure that they're in control, and the aim is complete control. This means that your reality will be tarnished in order to make you believe everything they say from their mouths. But of course, there's a chance that there's a problem, it's not true.

They'll use what you love as Ammo

It happens often when dealing with someone who is child who is a bit confused about what a parent to children is. They are fond of using the children as ammo. They might do it with other things

86

as well. If you're a lover of your pet and they love you, they will use it to make ammo. When you've got a loved one that is important to you They'll realize how important they are to you and that's the first thing they'll pick to take on.

If you're blessed with a family and they're not happy, perhaps they'll tell you that you shouldn't get so close to your familymembers, or that they take the pity of the way you look. When it comes to children and children, they'll openly say that you're not worthy to have children, and claim that you shouldn't be allowed to have them.

They'll try to smack your belt below the waist. They'll target your negative qualities that you are displaying and say that you're a suck and that you're doing everything wrong, and you're useless.

What is the reason you think they would do that? It is likely that they wish to take you down a notch or two until they get you to where you take everything that the abuser has to say as true. It's likely that you will begin to question whether you're being targeted since they'll target every single one of your sensitive areas even if you doubt they'll.

You're feeling anxious talking to them

If you are feeling this way when you talk to people there is a chance that you could be gaslights. Gaslighting is so pervasive, since they are aware of the fact that they could make you feel tired over time.

The remarks are snide and they'll make comments that aren't always in the same order, the whole thing is insidious But the ultimate goal is to gradually reduce your own strength and to tear you down.

The sad thing is that it's effective.

Anyone who has the power, strength, and capability to be aware of their thoughts and actions, can get caught in this trap, and that's why it's so terrifying. It's similar to the illustration of a frog trapped in an oil pan.

Have you thought of it? A similarity is when frogs get placed in a frying pan however the heat within it is gradually increased to the point that the frog isn't aware until the frying pan is cooked and crimped, when it's already too late.

It's not uncommon to not even realize that you're being victimized in this manner up until the moment it's all over which is the most terrifying aspect of gaslighting. It's one of the reasons why abusers continue to continue to do it for decades in the future.

Words and Actions Do Not Match With

Do you remember the saying that actions speak more than words? If you're working with someone that likes gaslights, you must be attentive to their actions instead of their words.

They'll do things that they usually are completely in opposition to what they really say.

"Oh I'd never ever talk to her and harm your feelings, dear"--Goes out and gets spotted with girls.

"I really love you dear"--Will absolutely denigrate your life

"I am truly concerned about you and would like that you live your best life"-- Will remove their daughter's clothes as well as different aspects that define their fashion.

It is usually seen typically with abusive boyfriends or parents who are abusive, as they'll say something and then perform another act and often find themselves repeating the same mistake to ensure that they are doing what they ought to be doing.

Of course, the aim is to confuse you , and to make you question whether there really is a real self to the person and if they really are the person they claim to be.

Uses Positivity to Confound You

This is something that lots of people do not know that will occur. They'll occasionally throw some positive energy to try and confuse you. They'll be complete a**holes to you, always trying to make the impression that you're not or putting you down, making you feel guilty They'll tell falsehoods and tell you that you're insane. Every occasionally they'll add a bit of positive reinforcement in the hope of trying to make you feel confused.

They'll slap you in the face and tell you they don't value you, and afterwards, they'll randomly praise your actions you take.

Why would they do this? Wouldn't it be more beneficial if you were simply scolded? The goal is to deceive you and cause you to feel uneasy.

They'd like you to believe that the person who is abusing you "isn't not that bad, isn't it?" and you start to let the victim be free to do whatever they want because they're nice to you once every once in awhile. They'll often attempt to convince you to reconsider the reality of your life and this is what they do. It is common to look back at the things that you have received praise for and usually, you can identify it as benefiting the gaslighters.

This is particularly true with narcissistic relationships. If you're a child of a narcissistic parent who constantly makes you feel slammed and ripped down and, often, are dismissed as nothing. However, sometimes, there's an ounce of "hey it's not so bad, you're not really a shit" that they show you. This is because you performed something they were pleased with or did something that they felt was beneficial to them. It is also common for them to attempt to add some of their personal 2 cents to it by saying that it was their fault that helped and that's the reason you're very accomplished.

You're confused and weak

Confusing is the main goal. Why is this? It's because confusion is the way people weaken.

They understand how stable people are looking for. They would like the regularity, the routine that comes with it. However, they'd like to totally unroot it and challenge every single thing that occurs. Of course there is a instinct to see the person who can help you feel more secure and see them as someone who one can depend on whenever things get tough.

Who do they go to? It's the person who's in the middle of their saga.

They'd like to create it seem like you're lost there's no place to turn and the only option is to be slighted. They don't want you to feel safe and secure, so they'll try everything to ensure that you don't.

Projection and Projection!

Projection is the mainstay of these kinds. We'll get further into this later However, they are experiencing the mental dissonance and projection that the majority of abusive and negative people experience.

They'll say that you're cheating, or that they're stealing things or items, and they'll basically say that you're guilty of something.

If you begin to be blamed, you'll see yourself trying to justify yourself it's all about you. Sometimes, they'll attempt to make you believe that you're the person doing everything, causing an internal guilt-based system inside you.

Who is the true cheat in this case? Who is the true abuser?

It's the gaslight.

They'll immediately begin to blame you, with the intent to take the blame and placing the blame on someone else. These are those who have been who cheat. However, each time you confront them about it or even confront them, they is returned to you in one way or another.

Other People Aren't Against You

Don't believe that they're simply pursuing you now and are only looking to take down you. They are actually adept at manipulating those they know will be close to regardless of what and will use to harm you.

If, for instance, an egotistical mother is smirking at you, it's likely that she has an "golden child" who is able to do nothing wrong, and is flawless which she will immediately to manipulate and use against you. They'll make statements that suggest that they know they are wrong or that you're insignificant and they won't trust you. They might, however, have never even spoken to anyone regarding you. Or perhaps they've never ever said anything and, of course they lie and will continue to lie.

Gaslighters will use this method to create a situation where you don't know who your friend or foe you are, and who you can count on. The intention is to make you realize that nobody is trustworthy and that you should remain with the gaslighters.

Of course, this will give them precisely what they want, plus more control. They would like you to return to the gaslight and, as you'll discover, also, there's a lot that is a consequence of this. In the end, you may feel as if your family members hate you.

Sometimes, narcissistic mothers and stepparents may turn to around on one part of their family on the other and claim that the other dislikes you and doesn't want to meet you. However, this isn't actually the situation. In fact, if you get in touch with them again they may say that's not the case and that they're wrong.

And of course, you can be thankful for your gaslight for this.

You Feel Freaky

They might tell you straight that you're insane, or they might tell others they think you're insane.

It's one of the most effective tools used by them because they are the way they do it is very dismissive. Sometimes, they will in a straightforward manner claim that the person is insane and shouldn't be trusted, and that you shouldn't trust them. They are smirked as they say the words will know that you're likely not even think about the statement.

Naturally, when person in question questions the gaslight and questions you about it, they will not trust you because they're aware that when you claim that the gaslight is a snide, it's completely out of your hands, and it's a great tactic.

Feels jealous, and thinks Everyone is lying

If you see that someone else says they're not happy about being gaslighted or that everyone else is lying Then it's time that you left the room and realized that you're dealing.

The idea behind this is that after you have told the person who is being victimized that all the rest of us are lying Guess what happens to you? It forces you to think about your own truth obviously! It's not often that you meet someone who has the guts (or insanity) to commit this type of thing. Obviously it's not your fault, and it's real, isn't it? But it's not. They'll claim that everyone lies and that everyone else is doing got it wrong, and that gaslight is the sole one who has the correct information.

"Oh do not believe in your friends. They're lying. They don't know me at all."

"Your grandmother is a deranged bitch, she clearly has the wrong idea, and she's losing her sanity. So don't believe her."

"It's for your own safety not to believe your mother. She's a scumbag and lies constantly on everything."

They'll claim that others are lying and that they are able to make a fool of themselves However, the truth of the matter is that you're the one confronted with a grade A liar and the one who must take on the aftermath of the liar's actions.

Gaslighters are likely to be lying to turn your back on them as, well they're all lying isn't it?

You begin to feel like you are about to Slowly You Feel Yourself Start To Slowly Die

I'm not always speaking physically about this issue. This is, however, one of the most obvious signs of gaslighting you begin to experience. It's not long before you begin becoming aware that you're changing into someone totally different.

This is more evident than any other aspect of the level of confidence you possess. The victims of gaslighting appear to have a loss of confidence. What's frightening is that any of the most confident people can turn into an empty shell of the person they once were. The worst part is that they may not even be aware of what's taking place.

Victims will begin to shrink in relation to their own situation, which means they'll only behave in ways that favor the gaslighter.

This is why people who have been victims of narcissistic abuse may adopt the characteristics of the perpetrator. Certain people who are judged by other people will adopt the characteristics of the other person , or might even be yes-men because they are unsure of what to do.

It's a sad thing when this happens, which is the reason why if you are able to leave your narcissistic lover, you will begin to feel more at ease and more authentic, and much more content in the end.

These are the obvious symptoms of gaslighting. If you suspect that you are witnessing gaslighting it is time to begin making a change. It's terrifying, but it's also possible to get out, particularly in the

event that your own mental health is at
risk.

Chapter 8: What to Do to Stop Gaslighting Abuse

In every gaslighting incident there is an upside. In a relationship like this it takes two people to dance. The influence your gaslighter has over you, the target, will only come valid as long as you let him to. While it's certainly difficult to break out of the relationship, it's precisely what you have to do. Gaslighters aren't your typical diplomats. This means that they're not intelligent. Therefore, stop trying to argue with them. Even though it may appear that you don't have the option to walk away, remember that you definitely can. You may have been told that no one would take you seriously, or that they're just trying to tolerate your behavior. This is just an attempt to keep you within the relationship and under their supervision. Be aware that you could opt-out. If you decide to remain and fight their snarky behavior you should do it on your own terms.

Gaslighting abuse is a result of the victim wishes to remain and convince her gaslighter to view things from her own viewpoint. Why is this desperate effort to convince the gaslighter to her side? Because she is desperate to gain his support. It's life-sustaining for them. His approval will make her feel complete again. This approval signifies that she is able to finally allow him to accept her own reality. This is a huge victory for her if she can accomplish this feat. After a series of misrepresentations to the truth this proves that she isn't insane or deluded as she was made to appear. Be assured that this isn't going to occur. The gaslighting effect was apparent as he managed to subvert your perception of reality. He's just not able to soft-pedal. This means that his grip on you is broken. Who would be the Magician who knowingly lets the spell he casts over his target to be broken? Accepting your sense of perception cuts off the whole control plan and power game he's involved in.

You don't require the approval of your partner to be complete. You are just who you are. There is no need for anyone's approval to be human.

You must also not excuse your gaslighting and not take any advice from them. Don't justify their failures. If they've failed in their duty and acted, they have to accept the blame.

In addition, you'll have to establish limits on what is acceptable to you as well as what's unacceptable. This should never be played with. It helps you get a feel of what you're willing accept and helps you understand the way that your gaslighter sees you. If he has crossed this red line multiple times without a single worry it is time to opt out of the whole thing.

You are able to trust your own perception of reality. If your gaslighter doesn't align with your viewpoint be sure to take your opinion with a pinch salt. Be awestruck by what you listen to and don't let the opinion of your gaslighter to overshadow your own. If he realizes that you're not trusting his claims or opinions anymore, he'll begin to reverse. In this case it could be that he decides to end the relationship of the basis of his own choice.

Last but not least, be sincere to yourself. Examine your relationship in depth to determine where you are at right now. Do you require therapy? Are you able to handle the abuse? can manage by yourself? Are you satisfied? Do you feel you need to stop the way that he keeps putting you down? The answers to these and a host of other questions you'll be asking will help you determine what most appropriate next step to follow. Remember, you have the only leverage you have You can always take a step back.

Chapter 9: The Emotional Manipulation Narcissism

What is the work of the puppeteer? It's just the manipulating and controlling of puppets. Nothing more, no less. The person who is the puppeteer isn't at all in love with their marionettes or their puppets. They do not care about making the puppet live in real life; rather their joy is watching the puppet do exactly what is instructed. If the marionette dances it's a jig. If it cry, laughs or anything else that is not a puppeteer's fault, then the puppeteer is in charge. Because it's an object, it is unable to think on its own. The puppet is a reflection of the imagination of the puppeteer.

What does the puppeteer have to do with manipulating emotions? This is how it all is interconnected. Emotional manipulative (also known as psychological abuse) is a type of abuse in which one is forced to treat another that may result in

105

depression, anxiety, extreme fear, complete or partial submission self-doubt and other psychological traumas. This kind of abuse could be applied in various situations including workplace relations, personal relationships, as well as other human rights abuses (including torturing). The main concern in this book is the way that emotional manipulation or abuse can be employed in social situations (personal relationships) and in the workplace.

The work of an emotional manipulator is similar to the work of the role of a puppeteer (by by the way, there's no problem with doing puppeteering!). The perpetrator aims to take the control of their victim, and influence them to perform exactly what they want (the same way that a puppeteer would). Being a victim's lover or not does not matter for an emotional manipulator, they're not interested in making the victim feel good. Instead, their main concern and enjoyment is watching their victim (their puppet) perform to their wishes and exaggerations. The manipulator of emotions is enthralled by creating the victim as an extension of their own imagination.

It can manifest as gaslighting, sexism, rejection and threats to speak and in many instances it could lead to physical violence, particularly in relationships with family members. The consequences from emotional abuse may be damaging and can leave victims feeling demoralized and deprived of self-esteem.

However, if emotional abusers are so horrible people, why would a rational person choose to enter into relationships with them? The first thing to consider is that the sane don't go into relationships with emotionally abusive individuals because they have a knack of concealing their motives right in the beginning. They lure innocent victims to their abode and try their best to keep them there by convincing their victims they hold some kind influence over them. There are certain warning signs are typically visible from the beginning to anyone who is attentive. However, people who are good-natured (who make up many of the people who have been victims of abuse emotionally) tend to ignore the warning signs. This is especially true when it comes to romantic relationships. They will quickly dismiss these red flags using beautiful excuses, such as, "Love overlooks a multitude of mistakes!"

There are many types of emotionally abusive people. Not all are created equal. Many of them will change over time (but it's not your obligation to alter them). But, some manipulators are suffering from a mental disorder known as Narcissistic personality disorder (NPD).

Understanding Narcissism

An emotional abuser is thought to be suffering from an narcissistic personality disorder if their behavior is consistent and affects the way they interact with others. This can make it difficult to manage criticism or negative feedback. They often interpret criticism as threatening, which they respond to by feeling humiliated and resenting others, launching into rage and disdainful towards other people.

A person who has NPD is arrogant, proud and pretentious. They are constantly seeking to be appreciated and an exaggerated feeling of superiority. They may think that other people are jealous of them, and they're always jealous of the accomplishments of others. NPD's have a feeling of entitlement. They think that other people have a right to preferential treatment. They're quick to compare themselves to other people who are inferior and are more likely to associate with those who they believe to be superior because they are.

A narcissist can dominate conversations and become the focus of attention. They are driven with beauty, success and power and want to be the highest quality of what they are involved in. They're not aware of the needs and feelings of others and frequently devise strategies to exploit individuals and situations to gain own gain.

The causes of Narcissism

There isn't a known reason for narcissism. However, its symptoms are frequently related to:

Background and education The setting and the parenting style are often the main factors that influence the way that people live their lives. Parents and caregivers that show overly affection or care of their children can lead to the notion that the child is entitled to be treated with respect by all. Additionally the constant parental criticism and indifference can cause negative consequences on the child's psychological well-being and affect them when they become adults.

Genetics: The inheritance of traits from parents can cause the narcissistic behavior of an individual.

Neurobiology: This refers the way that a person's brain (and brain) creates and processes their perceptions, thoughts and the way that it influences their behavior.

Signs of Narcissism

Only an expert can tell whether someone is suffering from NPD. Certain signs can indicate possible abuse regardless of whether or not the person is an person who is a narcissist. Therefore, look for these indicators and if you observe a pattern in someone, it's recommended to stay clear of any relationship with them, or to find ways to break up your relationship if you're already in a relationship with one.

They aren't comfortable apology: A clear sign of narcissism is that they are always right. Whatever everyone calls an argument, for a narcissist, is the conversation. This makes it nearly impossible to provide apology because they are simply declaring what they think of things from their perspective (which is often the only legitimate viewpoint). The word remorseful has been taken out of their dictionary.

Empathy is a foreign concept to them Narcissists are generally difficult to empathize. It's not their thing which is why they can't connect with people in a more profound way. If you're seeking people who can share your thoughts with you, who can know where you're and where you are coming from, narcissists do not belong in the list! Your worries, fears, and how difficult your day was relevant to them.

The tendency to love-bomb you when a narcissist thinks the person "up in their eyes," they can shower with praise, admiration gifts, and displays of affection and love. They seem to appear too strong and will declare their love for you , even when you don't know each other well. In no time, they're exhausted because nobody can really live up to their expectations and the love-bomb transforms into an emotional nightmare.

They do not have (or have only a handful of) long-term relationships it is hard for narcissists to make long-term friendships. They are only able to remain close to someone the duration of time they require some kind of support from them.

Avoiding a relationship that is committed
If someone is preventing you from interacting with others, but they do not be a committed partner in a relationship with you, then they might keep you in order to fulfill their sexual desires. They aren't concerned in flirting with others however they are fast to be apprehensive when you do something related to flirting.

Different types of Narcissistic Abuse

Most people think that a narcissist will be someone who is threatening and dangerous but that isn't often the situation. If you aren't aware of the various types and shades of these behavior It is easy to be deceived into inviting one into your lives. The first step in keeping the narcissists from your life is to never dismiss any warning signs you spot. Don't let someone's charming side keep you from their narcissistic behaviours.

Here's a brief explanation of the various kinds of narcissists, as well as their different forms of abuse.

The Narcissist Who Bullies A narcissist who is bully-like doesn't use bully tactics for the same reasons like a normal bully. Normal bullies attack other people due to struggling with self-doubt and want to be accepted by society. Narcissists do similar things since they are satisfied feeling that others are suffering. Most often the bully is a regular one who uses physically abusive and overt threats to their victims. A bully narcissist adopts more of an emotional approach, rather than an physical one. They employ an even more devious technique to intimidate their victims. This is known as gaslighting, a sly method of bullying that causes victims to believe they're insane. A gaslighter is a self-absorbed bully who does not feel any remorse when other people are injured through their actions, actions, and even their words. They deliberately make others feel as if they are a complete jerk because they are in charge of others' lives.

The Toxic Narcissist They are among the most savage kinds of Narcissists. They can cause emotional pain or drama on others.

Narcissists who are toxic can react in a way that is unpredictable when others don't pay them the respect and attention they want. They may even cause people to lose their jobs, relationships, or even physically harm other people. Some narcissists won't take the time to hurt others However, the toxic narcissist has an issue with hounding others and causing them serious harm.

The Narcissist with an Exhibitionist Style: These are the self-centered, arrogant and self-centered narcissists that ensure that everyone else around them is aware that they're Narcissists. They are the centre of attention and go to any lengths to get noticed.

It is the Seducer Narcissist: In contrast to typical narcissistic traits seducer narcissist is able to give compliments and even perform actions to make others feel better about themselves (for example, love-bombing people). They may even be dependent, but not for long. When they have what they want and they'll drop you like hot potatoes! For intimate relationship, as an instance seducer narcissists can make all kinds of nice comments to convince their target to have sexual relations with them only to abandon them immediately following. They can also trick other people into a relationship in order to show they are able to date any person they wish.

The Closet Narcissist The Closet Narcissist: They are the most difficult kind of narcissists that you can spot. In contrast to other narcissists that demand attention and can cause chaos within the lives of other people They employ more subtle methods. They are able to put on an act of selflessness. However, because they are not truly compassionate They are motivated by the desire to receive praise or be appreciated. They also possess an uncanny feeling of being entitled.

The Psychopathic Narcissist The Psychopathic Narcissist: These are the most violent narcissists. They're unstable, unpredictable and extremely violent.

There is no way to know for certain if someone is a psychopathic Narcissist since they are more easily identifiable. The media often portrays the psychopathic narcissists as the model for all things narcissistic. This makes many people unaware of the characteristics of other kinds of narcissists.

How Do You Know If You're Being Abusive Emotionally

It's a lot more easy to identify emotional abuse when you're not the one being abused. However, when you're in the middle It becomes a completely totally different ballgame. There are multiple moving parts to allow you to be able to see what's happening under your nose. You're fighting between your feelings, emotions as well as your confused thoughts and perceptions, and at the same time , trying to understand the implications of your actions on your spouse, you and the relationship. All of this could make you quickly miss the symptoms of abusive behavior.

117

There are a variety of ways an individual can hurt you emotionally. Some of the most well-known methods include:

Then they will control and shame you.

The emotional abuse may be a form of making you feel ashamed of your weaknesses, losing confidence in yourself. It is done through:

• Financial Control - requiring you provide a full budget and limiting access to funds. They attempt to force you to demand money, and could even have bank accounts under sole their name.

* Threats , both overt and undercover threats. They could make statements such as "You have no idea what you can accomplish." They might also threat to kidnap the children and take them to some unknown place.

* issuing orders - demanding you to perform certain actions, regardless of regardless of whether it's appropriate or not.

You are treated like an adult - making decisions about your clothes or what

118

friends you keep, what food items you are allowed to take in, where you can go and many more.

Monitors and spying appearing without notice to ensure that you're who you declare to be. They might insist that you answer messages and calls immediately no matter if it's practical or not. They may even look through your text messages, call logs email messages, and request the passwords you use on social networking sites.

• Making decisions that are not consulted with you , such as unintentionally cancelling appointments or closing a joint bank account, and even talking directly to your boss without having you ask first.

The unpredictable emotional behavior of a person that make it difficult to know when they will move next. At one point, they're showering you with love, and the next they are screaming in a way that is uncontrollable. It is impossible to predict the next time they will be.

Critiquing or pointing out the negative, as well as humbling You

The perpetrators of emotional abuse employ these strategies to constantly lower confidence in yourself. No matter if the issue is large or small issue, you're being slapped with harsh punishments like:

* Name-calling - calling you derogatory pet-names. They might employ harsh phrases to describe you like dumb, stupid irresponsible, a fool, an incompetent an utter loser, a disappointing, incompetent lazy, etc.

Talking about your appearance using defamatory language for your look or attire.

* Distancing - making you feel unprepared to figure things out. For instance, "Oh sweet darling, I can tell you're doing your best however this is way not within your grasp."

* Yelling - attempting to intimidate you through swearing at, screaming, or yelling at you in order to make you feel

inadequate. They might throw objects or punch their fists for more impact.

* Character assassination that makes people feel that they "always" act in a way that is not acceptable. For instance, "You are always wrong," or, "You constantly mess up things!"

* Pushing your buttons speaking and doing things they know will make you angry.

* Releasing your achievements by denying your accomplishments or claiming credit for your accomplishments.

Isolation and Neglect of Emotions

This is accomplished by putting your emotional requirements to the back of the line as the abuser's needs are the top priority. It is a situation where you are emotionally stranded as the abuser will take away any emotional support that you could get from other people , and then force you to rely on them. However, they eventually stop giving you any emotional assistance. If you feel you have an excessive amount of emotional needs that are not being met it is likely that you are to be in a toxic relationship. The effects of emotional neglect and isolation may manifest in these ways:

* Refraining affection, which includes physical contact and sexual relationships.

* Do not communicate with you - clearly refusing to contact your via verbal communication, textmessages, emails, phone calls or in any other way.

* Discriminatory treatment that is not focusing on you, totally disregarding you, or even looking at something else while talking to you.

* Keeping your from socializing and making excuses for about why you shouldn't get involved with your friends socially.

* Turning off you by completely disinteresting you, shifting the topic or ignoring you when you wish to discuss a topic.

* Refraining you from your family members - using excuses to explain why you can't attend family gatherings.

* Interrupting your conversation - calling your attention when you're in middle of talking to someone else or talking on the phone.

* Being uninterested - showing that you are not concerned about the pains or injuries you suffer.

Insinuating, Blaming and Outright Denial

The emotional abusers suffer from deep-seated fears which they attempt to hide by showing a display of control in public. One method of covering their anxiety is by blame or accusing others of the things they did or said. This could take forms like:

* Turning the tables against you , blaming them for their frustration and issues with control.

* False allegations of abuse, suggesting you're the person with anger and control issues, or making someone else the target.

* Making excuses for your negative jokes and creating the impression that you're incapable of taking an oath even if the joke is personal to you.

123

* Denial: losing, damaging, concealing or damaging something belonging to you, and denying any knowledge about it.

* They're guilt-tripping you, creating the impression that you are owed something. They're quick to highlight the numerous favors they've performed for you.

* Refuting their abusive behavior and feigning shock at the thought of being labeled an abuser.

• Denying discussions and agreements - burning you to raise questions about your mental sanity and memory. The emotional abusers will blatantly claim that they never agreed to do something, or ever engaging in a debate over things.

Bottom Line

A relationship that is abusive can be a burden on your life and make you question your mental sanity. However, the longer you continue to doubt yourself, the more serious and more messed up the damage becomes. Removing yourself from emotional abuse isn't an easy feat however, it is possible to do it. A very harmful kinds of emotional abuse is gas lighting. It can be very difficult to overcome since it alters your self-confidence and perceptions. Luckily, the rest of this book focuses on demonstrating how you can escape the traps to gas light.

Chapter 10: The Repercussions of Gaslighting

There are a myriad of possible outcomes that may occur when you are a victim of gaslighting. The victim may experience many different emotional and psychological states. Although there are numerous consequences that could occur but we will examine the three that are the most frequently seen. We will go over each of them in detail to help you gain a better comprehension of what you could feel if you or a loved one has been gaslighted.

The initial effect is very frequent is disbelief. Gaslighting, as we've said, is extremely emotional abuse, and can be used to manipulate another. When gaslighting occurs the victim begins to lose faith actually, their convictions and judgment.

Most of the time the first reaction to the gaslighting tactics is the one of doubt. The victim won't be capable of wrapping their brains about the sudden shift in behavior targeted at them. They'll likely be completely shocked by the very realisation that they're being slighted. The victim is likely to be aware that something terrible is taking place within relationships, however it's extremely unlikely that they'll be able to identify the exact cause. This is clearly the aim of the gaslighter who is narcissistic.

The narcissistic gaslighter set the stage for their objective right from the beginning. They'll get the victim to fall in love with their charms hook, line and sinker. A victim may believe there is love between them and the gaslighter since they've been seduced. They will truly believe that love is truly being expressed by both of them even though it is not the case.

It happens because, at the beginning, interactions between the narcissist and victim will be great. They will be working together to achieve mutual goals, and everything will be right. Then the gaslighter starts making the victim wait or diverting them.

The victim will be held to the fact that the relationship are between themselves and their selfish companion or at one point were good.

They are unable to comprehend why their loved one is becoming extremely negative and critical with regard to them. The once loving and supportive relationship has now become one of resentment and pain.

However much gaslighting being conducted be aware that the consequences could be serious for the person who is the victim. Gaslighting strategies can be subtil, making difficult to identify. Because of the subtlety involved in gaslighting, confidence is eroded without the victim even realizing. The victim eventually is unable to believe in themselves as they believe what their narcissistic friend is constantly telling them.

The confusion is often accompanied by doubt. The gaslighter might move things and then lie about how they were the ones who did it which makes the victim doubt their own sanity. It's a game for the narcissist. It is one of psychological conflict. They might say things, but when you ask them to completely deny it to ask for assistance. The victim may begin questioning their memories as well as the way they see their experiences throughout their lives. They'll begin to look for the approval of the egocentric gaslighter. They hope to be assured that they aren't going insane. This means they are extremely dependent on their abusers as they believe they are the sole source of reality.

Another consequence of gaslighting is that the victim becoming defensive. It is typical to Ward in the beginning, when the victim has enough self-worth to fight back against the tactics employed by the gaslighter who is narcissistic. Most of the time, when one gets defensive, it's already too late, as the motives of the gaslighter have begun to be realized. They aim to cause their victims to become unstable. They attempt to create anxiety, guilt and self-doubt inside the victim.

Through the creation of these negative feelings the narcissistic gaslighter causes harm to the victim's mental state. In time the victim begins to question their reality and even themselves. It can cause feeling confused and lost. They won't believe that they are able to trust their memories or instincts. When this happens it is probable that the person will become isolated themselves. They will attempt to avoid contact with others as they feel a sense of shame, guilt, and depression.

The effects of gaslighting can eventually make the victim ineffective to take on the narcissistic partner within their relationships. Because they'll eventually not be capable of defending themselves, they put themselves at risk of losing themselves completely. The harm caused can affect the person on a physical, mental as well as emotional scale.

Stockholm syndrome is a different ill-effect of gaslighting. The traditional Stockholm syndrome happens the time when someone who is kidnapped or held hostage starts to believe or feel a sense of affection towards their hostage. When it comes to narcissistic gazlighting, it is different. The person who is victimized isn't necessarily being forced to do something however, at the same at the same time, they are a victim of the manipulation and harm that gaslighting causes.

The ongoing psychological and emotional assault that is caused by gaslighting may leave the victim feeling like they can't live without their narcissistic partner. They begin to look at the person who is who is abusing them to seek acceptance and love. They are unable to recognize that the person they're looking to is actually the one who is creating harm for them. They all have similar symptoms from Stockholm syndrome.

Our brains are designed to safeguard ourselves at a fundamental level, even if the protection is due to retreating. If the person is trying to cope with the traumatic situation of the narcissist in their life, they'll go to extreme lengths in order to connect to their abuser. It helps in reducing the cognitive dissonance that they are experiencing.

This bond by the person who is the perpetrator and victim is usually very difficult to break.

This is why it is often observed that individuals will remain in narcissistic, abusive relationships. Strategies for survival come in numerous forms and this is an excellent illustration of one our subconscious minds may select.

Depression is another major result of gaslighting. When a victim is in depression, it is extremely difficult to look into the mirror and see them. They'll likely be feeling like just a shadow of who they once were. They live under constant stress and an ever-present state of anxiety. They will be totally at ease.

If a person is depressed the person's mental and emotional state is not healthy. It is probable that they won't be able to make their own decisions. They may feel that they lack motivation, confidence or happiness in their lives. The fear of being unable to perform their duties correctly will become so regular that they won't be able to trust in their self-generated opinions.

When this mentality has been established the victim, it is likely the victim will become detached from the activities and friends they used to enjoy. Their whole perception of reality will be altered to the point of being tragically delusional. Instead of trying to find to overcome the depression, they will see the depression as a means of escape.

It is crucial to remember that many individuals who have extreme levels of gaslighting may end up with post-traumatic stress disorder. Based on the symptoms that are evident, this diagnosis might be detected. The symptoms of PTS are classified into three categories. These categories are:

Reliving the past: This can include nightmares, flashbacks, anxiety, and images that are intrusive.

Avoidance: Examples are staying away from certain locations and people or even thoughts, or becoming emotionally numb and feeling depressed or a lack of interest in everything.

Arousal: Among the signs of the arousal process are problems with concentration and concentrating, higher levels of irritability, anger outburst, insomnia or waking up, and hyper-vigilance.

The final issue we'd like to talk about is known as the narcissistic victim syndrome. There's not a great deal of research conducted on this condition yet, however, it is something that is going to be studied. People who are affected by this disorder have suffered from extreme levels of harm to themselves from a gaslighter who is narcissistic.

Sometimes, they aren't aware of what happened to them until they begin talking to an expert. When the story has been told and they are aware of what happened to them and their family, they might feel a sense of shock, sadness or guilt, doubt and anger.

If you are suffering from Narcissistic Victim Syndrome may have similar symptoms to those who suffer from Post-Traumatic Stress Disorder. They may experience flashbacks of their abuser as well as panic attacks, severe levels of anxiety, fatigue, disassociation thoughts, and possibly eating disorders. Even with the negative effects there are many who experience a sense relief from knowing what been their experience. This information allows people to move toward healing and confronting the trauma.

It's surprising how resilient human beings can be. Be aware that even if you suffer from the consequences of narcissistic shaming, things are likely to improve. It's going to require some effort to identify yourself again , and to be in a position to release the hurt resulted from your victim's narcissism. Making contact with your family, friends as well as professionals can assist in making the journey of healing much easier.

The process of dealing with all the negative consequences can be very lonely.

It is widely believed that there aren't many people out there who suffer the same experience and struggling to make it through However, you'll be shocked at how many people's lives have been ruined through gaslighting. In addition, it's remarkable how many people bounce back to live happy, healthy and fulfilled lives.

Whatever the length of time you've been suffering from the narcissistic gaze, there is an option that will be taken to get you out of it. It requires courage and a strong support system to build the courage to step away from your narcissistic sexy abuser. When you are able to achieve this, you'll make the first step to the path of recovery. The consequences of narcissistic abuse can last for an extremely lengthy time, but there are many ways to cope that will help you overcome them.

In the next book, we'll examine various strategies that you can employ to deal with narcissistic gazetting and its effects. There are many sources available to aid you on the difficult process of healing. The most important thing to keep in mind is that regardless of how difficult things got you can always make them better with focus, investigation and help.

Chapter 11: The Gaslighting Effect

Gaslighting is one form of psychological abuse where the perpetrator constantly accuses the victim of doing or saying something they were not aware of.

What they say or do creates extreme anxiety for the victim. They question their memory or perception and judgement. The people who employ the gaslighting method intend to alter the victim's story in order to allow them to accept the reality they are handed onto them in the form of their personal. The gaslighting technique, which is commonly employed by dictators, is effective when a lie that is presented frequently enough, is accepted as truth.

As per Darlene Lancer JD, LMFT of Psychology Today: "Gaslighting is an illegal and concealed type of psychological and emotional abuse that is de-signed to sow seeds of self-doubt as well as alter the perception of real life." 27

Everyone can be affected by gaslighting from any aspect of life. It occurs in a variety of relationships, such as families, friends or colleagues, as well as romantic partners. The nature of gaslighting is that you can not truly comprehend it until you've experienced it yourself and, even then, it's difficult to believe it.

Gaslighting is a form of bad behavior intended to trigger emotional reactions and destabilize the primary frame of an individual's mental balance. These responses are amplified and then used to depict the victim as insane, insane, or an abuser. The victim is conditioned to believe that they are the culprit and accept the blame for the anger of the abuser and believes they be the cause of their behavior to be the cause as a way to justify their savage, cruel actions. There is no way to comprehend someone deliberately harming them without cause They believe they are the cause. Normal people do not understand the kind of violence that is happening. It's outside the realm of reason, and they aren't able to comprehend what's happening to them, and struggle to explain the situation. The victims are aware that something is wrong.

Narcissists thrive on emotions, which is why they create every scenario possible to trigger emotional responses.

The phrase "gaslighting" is derived from the play of 1938 created by Patrick Hamilton that made the silver screen in 1944, in George Cukor's film "Gaslight". Ingrid Bergman played a young beautiful girl called Paula who was witness to her mother's murder at the family home. Later, Paula would go on to marry a narcissist Gregory (Charles Boyer) and then return to the home of her family in which her mother was murdered.28

As time passes, Paula begins to doubt her own sanity , as her husband attempts to convince her that she is losing her memory and becoming emotionally explosive that she's gone insane. He will moving pictures, dim lighting and bang against the walls to convince her she's lost her mind, and that she is dreaming about the whole thing. 29

The term is derived from a film, its definition is simple: when lies are repeated in confidence and the victim begins questioning their sense of sanity and believes the lies to be true. As a result, Stockholm Syndrome is also a symptom as the victim becomes unsure that they can discern reality and is looking at the narcissistic gaze-lighter to get their perspective, forming an intense trauma-based attachment.30

Narcissists who employ the gaslighting technique are hurt and angry. They appear to be the victim when they are confronted or challenged. The covert manipulation can easily turn into a blatant abuse, with accusations directed at the victim that state they are ungrateful, distrustful or disrespectful. emotionally sensitive, overly sensitive insensitive, dishonest emotionally damaged, unsecure useless, and so on. The abuse can escalate into outrage and intimidation, which can be and be followed by threats, punishment or intimidation in the event that the perpetrator doesn't believe the lies they're trying to convey to the victim.

The repeated lies and lies of the narcissist's character are likely to be accepted by the person who is being victimized as being true this is known as the illusion of truth and is at the root of all gaslighting.

Gaslighting is in essence an illusion of truth called the illusory-truth effect first noticed in the work of Hasher, Goldstein, and Toppino (1977). They observed that subjects were more likely to believe repeated statements likely to be true than statements that were new. Repetition is not a valid basis for truth. Wittgenstein observed that the tendency to believe in repeated statements to buying a new newspaper to determine whether the first one was true. Although repeated reading does not offer proof of truth, it can increase the likelihood of being familiar with. So, when lies are presented in a consistent manner, the victims could be enticed to accept it as truth. That's why the illusion of truth can be extremely efficient. 31

The victim's abuser would like their self-worth to drop by hoping they will feel a sense of inadequacy with their savage verbal attacks, subtle innuendos and twisted mental games. Certain victims are prone to believing in an untrue self-fulfilling prophecy once they begin to feel exactly like the person they're painting as. When they begin to think about and imagine many negative things about themselves the self-image disappears.

The whole premise for gaslighting lies in projection, a lie transforms into truth, then truth is a lie, and the narcissist keeps in the process of accusing victims of things that they're not doing, like lying, cheating, playing games and so on. This popular technique of manipulation is often referred to as"preemptive strike. As per Stephanie A. Sarkis, Ph.D. of Psychology Today, the narcissist shifts all blame onto

143

the victim, taking the focus off of the actual actions they are doing.32

This tactic of manipulation is efficient because , when someone is accused by the other of doing what the gaslighter really is doing and the victim is placed in a position in which they are required to prove which never took place. This can cause an emotional imbalance for the victim who is seeking to justify something that didn't take place, and they have very little time to concentrate on the gaslighting of the narcissist. 33

As per Sarkis, "Gaslighters, people who seek to control others by manipulating them, often blame others for actions they engage in. This is a common technique for manipulating others." 34

The narcissist could make it appear as if the victim is wrong by presenting false evidence to support their assertion. They also tend to omit details in their descriptions of events in order to make it appear different from what actually occurred. The people who are misled by the manipulative narcissist will get caught up in the drama and be enticed to the narcissist's constant stream of prefabricated, juicy discussions and events which never happened. place.35

The purpose of gaslighting is to harm the victim's self-esteem, self-confidence as well as their emotional mental state so that they can no longer function on their own but become increasingly dependent on their abuser's approval to prove their existence. When it is done well over time, can lead victims to fall into a state of submission and feelings feeling of worthlessness.

Gaslighting can take place in a variety of methods.

Since narcissists enjoy chaos and strife, they'll attempt to do anything to cause problems. This is done with the intent to continue the problem throughout the length of time they can that reduces and weakens emotionally the victim. To justify their savage and obnoxious attacks, they'll say that the victim caused the issue.

Innuendoes that include "silly you must have lost your memory," or "no, you didn't tell me about that," and "you told me last night, do you remember" frequently lead victims to believe that they are being diagnosed with dementia or have slipped into Alzheimer's disease because they're the primary target in their bizarre experience.

Some narcissists do not care about how they show they are dating other women and the victim is thrown out of control emotionally as they laugh and play with their indiscretions while creating a negative image of the person they are attempting to abuse. If they are confronted, it can give the narcissist that emotional reaction they want, and they'll continue to do it and give the victim no opportunity to escape their violence. The narcissist is constantly denial of any wrongdoing, while making sure that the victim believes that they are all lying to themselves.

The Reid interrogation technique is a method of gaslighting used in order to make up a fake perception or story to present for the person being questioned as truth. This might even be a full description of what the narcissist did or a lie they wish their victim to admit to. Victims are subjected to long hours of gruelling questions and answers such as, "Why did you do this?" or "Why are you lying about it? We are all aware of it." When statements like these are repeatedly asked in a row, the consequences can be fatal. A victim's defences get highthat they shake in fear to the the core of their being.

A narcissist delights by putting their victim under a microscope in public by displaying grandiose gestures of humiliation that are incredibly flirting with the staff serving them looking at inappropriately at the other sex and saying something that can upset the victim, or calling the victim in a way which is intended to trigger emotional outbursts, which support the narcissist's claims of mental illness to the public. The

147

victims are treated to silence as the environment is as frigid as ice every one of these actions is carefully planned by the person who is the narcissist. The narcissist might also choose to challenge the victim's spiritual side by stating, "I am God; you don't have to rely on HIM" or "you must get in touch in your relationship with God." It can cause the victim to doubt their faith. If this isn't enough they are left with the feeling that they're not worthy in the eyes of God. They are looking to attack the person's heart by removing their spirit, soul, and faith. Therefore, if God does not love them, then they are worthless, as the narcissist trying to depict. Making the victim feel guilty about their religion is the greatest achievement because the gaslighter is bound to want his victim to believe in him. Narcissists do not believe in God as they are too focused on believing that they are gods.

Stephanie A. Sarkis Ph.D. of Psychology Today, claims people who use gaslights typically use these techniques:

Telling blatant lies

They tell a simple straight-up lie while keeping a straight face in order to establish an example after having told an enormous lie. The victims don't know if they're ever told the truth, and this keeps their behavior off the mark.

Deny even though there's evidence

Narcissists could be found guilty of a crime, but they'll still have a excuse to justify it. There may be evidence to support them, but they'll still claim they were guilty.

Remove the foundation

They use the people closest to the victim as a weapon which includes their children and family members. They understand how important children and their families are for victims, and they could be the first targets they target. If the victim is a parent then the gaslighter may tell them that the person shouldn't have children.

Victim shaming

Narcissists can claim their victim is an insignificant person by citing many negative qualities so that other people will sympathize with the person who is confronting an "crazy or insane person."

They tear down their victim over time.

It is among the most esoteric aspects of gaslighting. It is carried out slowly, by slipping in the occasional lie and a casual comment occasionally before it begins getting more intense. Even the most intelligent, aware people are enticed into gaslighting, it's extremely efficient.

The actions of a narcissist are never in line with their actions and

In this instance, the actions speak more louder than words. They don't matter what they say, but it's the way they're doing which is the problem.

Positive reinforcement, which is intended to deceive the victim

The narcissist who slashes the victim is also able to build their character. Someone who has declared that the victim had no value now speaks of their worth. Most often, the value is the fact that the victim did something in order to protect the narcissist's interests.36

It begins with subtle mind games , such as planning and telling the victim that they didn't hear correctly or that the victim lies to them. It's a subtle, gradual procedure which leaves the victim lost and confused, wondering what transpired. Truth is altered when victims doubt their perception, reality and attitude They seek out the narcissist to get clarification and to ask why they're being treated in such a manner. Many victims believe that they will be able to get their abuser back with time, and then they'll appear nice and pleasant again. However, it is a fact that 'nice' does not happen when it is clear that the "cruel switch" is turned on. All niceties are solely a means to get the victim back to a good mood prior to another attack.

In this stage the narcissist has studied their victim for a long time to understand how to hit buttons to achieve the desired response. The gaslighting effect comes into full-force when they're criticized and the situation that was initially a sense of sympathy, it abruptly changed into disdain and animosity. In this moment, the victims' feelings are ignored, or their words are reduced or altered, which causes further confusion.

Narcissists thrive on conflict chaos, drama, and strife and will do everything to sustain it all the time they can. The entire experience can cause the victim to fall apart, as they become emotionally depressed. To justify their smug and savage behaviour, the narcissist may show their behavior to the victim, merely using phrases such as "you initiated the problem" or "it's due to you". When the victim is given an opportunity to relax and relax, the narcissist will take them to task. The cycle intensifies with time, and the narcissist causes the victim to lose all of their defense mechanisms.

At this stage, the narcissist is beginning to look for the weaknesses of their victim, which they believe are the result of sensitive emotions and human nature.

These emotions will be utilized to force the victim into controlled and planned responses.

The narcissist continues to alter the victim's perception of reality until it gradually is altered, giving the narcissist to claim "it's everything in your mind" or "you're too sensitive." The person who is a narcissist will not tolerate their own personal boundaries and will walk over them to achieve what they desire. In the mind of the narcissist, the victim is not permitted to express thoughts or views that are their own. Victims gradually begin to question what they do and say out of fear of being retaliated against by the narcissist. They also find it difficult to discern the truth from the fiction.

Shahida Arabi, bestselling author and graduated from Columbia University, claims narcissists use lies and partial truths to make the feelings of victims appear absurd, even though the only thing they're trying convey their feelings. This, she claims, "enables them to invalidate your right to express thoughts and feelings about their improper behavior , and also creates the feeling of guilt when you try to set boundaries."37

At first, the victims react to the shocking gaslighting in shock and disbelief. They cannot comprehend what's happening to the victims. They are aware that something is wrong, and that they're not being treated in a normal manner and aren't understanding what's happening, and that is precisely what the person who is gaslighting would like. If the victim was aware of the exact nature of what was happening to them, it would not be effective. This is the reason this kind of abuse works so well in disorienting the innocent victim.

Narcissists can also make use of their victim's weaknesses and embellish their own attempts to portray them as not quite perfect judge in their public opinion. The perpetrator will then make use of their position to appear to be the hero, while defending the victim from their own self-defence. This lets them justify their abuse to those who are not their. The narcissist has lulled their victims and other people to believe that the victim does not get the psychological torture which is in store for them.

The narcissist is mindful to not let their mask slide while making sure that all of the victim's family members and friends are like them. They'll then use the same system of support to make the victim feel weak by instilling doubt within the minds of the people who are closest to him or her. The objective is to create control over each individual, so that they are able to be eliminated in a series, leaving the victim on her own.

The narcissist now begins playing with the strings of their puppet and begin navigating his victim's surroundings in extraordinary ways. They are secretly taking away the foundation for the victims. They demolish all support systems by laying seeds of doubt. This is not just happening in the victim's own mind, but in every person the victim thinks they can count on. Friends, familymembers, and acquaintances suddenly behave differently towards the victim, without explanation this further disorients and causes confusion for the victim. The victim is having a difficult understanding why people appear to be changing their behavior without reason. Victims may cut people off due to the urging of the narcissist , or people begin to believe all the lies being spread by the Narcissist behind the victim's back and in either case the narcissist has succeeded in removing and isolating the victim.

The victims are so uncomfortable that they turn away from their beloved ones and begin to withdraw, eventually becoming lonely. As the victims withdraw and hide, the narcissist makes public displays to enhance their worth with people of the other sex, and often enjoy an evening out with a partner. This is the time when they're able to win the sympathy of others by in which they claim to be victims of a mentally sick partner who is to the home.

Chapter 12: What Causes Narcissism?

It is true that the Narcissus story is an well-known one to depict the self-absorption and ego of a narcissist. However there's not an in-depth discussion about the underlying causes of a full-blown personality disorders. There is no doubt in our society that narcissism is on the rise however, how exactly do they manifest as an illness of the personality? There are a variety of theories on the way narcissism manifests in an individual, starting from an initial "narcissistic wound" during childhood and a parent's story of devaluation and idealization, or even a neuroscientific perspective which focuses on how your brain works when you are a narcissist is affected by emotional and structural problems related to compassion (Kernberg 1975 Kohut 1971; Lavendar 2014; Schulze et . al 2013). (Kernberg, 1975; Kohut, 1971; Lavendar, 2014; Schulze et al., 2013). But as to the way

Narcissistic personality disorder develops within the individual There is no specific answer.

The Dr. Karen Bardenstein (2009) says in her book 'The Broken Mirror The Characteristics of Narcissistic Personality Disorder in Children in that, in the case of children who suffer from an illness, it is a matter of numerous factors that could be a risk. Narcissistic children typically are children of parents who are narcissistic adopted children who overindulge or challenged by their biological siblings from their adoptive parents children of parents who are successful especially when the child is not gifted with the same abilities as their parents, are overindulged, wealthy children, and children of divorce, in particular divorce where children do not have the same abilities like their parents.

Neglect of the physical or emotional As Kernberg (1975) suggests as a result of a parent who is critical Narcissists could have experienced trauma as young. The trauma of childhood that psychologists refer to as"a "narcissistic wound" could have caused to them, as a way of protecting themselves from harm, to block out the aspects of themselves that may connect with other people (Marks 2012; Lavender, 2014; De Lisle 2015). It could have been caused by a parent who scolded the child, made them feel abused and rejected their children, resulting in the phenomenon that Millon (1981) refers to as "compensatory narcissism,"" an illusion of self-protection that makes a child believe in a false sense of superiority in order to hide feelings of low self-worth.

At the opposite end of the spectrum theories that suggest that narcissism may be caused due to the child's self-esteem issues which allows the child to be an individual for the duration of its perceived superiority without consequences or any basis on the basis of empirical evidence. Instead of being devalued from a parent which could have caused a child to slow growth in their emotional development the pattern of overvaluation is in another way, the child is over-valued to the point that they acquire a attitude of entitlement and disdain for the emotions of others.

A study conducted in 2015 from The National Academy of Sciences Proceedings found that parents valued their children too much by telling them how unique were. Narcissism was predicted the words of the researchers, by parents' overvaluation and not due to the absence of warmth from parents. So, when parents internalize with their unrealistic expectations of their children (e.g."I have more power than other people and I have the right to be treated with advantages'), children tend to develop narcissism at least in the first place (Brummelman and. and al 2015).

This research confirms the notion that Randi Kreger (2012) describes as"the distinction" between "vulnerable" Narcissists and "great Narcissists." According to Kreger that grandiose narcissists have been nurtured by parents who bribe their children with confidence that they are their superiority and entitlement is while vulnerable narcissists appear to have the effect of reckless parenting.

As someone who taught young children with wealthy backgrounds I definitely saw an emerging sense of entitlement among parents who tolerated the conduct of their children, allowing their children to do what they want without apology to cross the rules of other people. Parents who gave their children a false belief in entitlement displayed an extremely sceptical behavior and, even when they did break the rules or abused their children in a way that was obscene and the ones who demonstrated to their children to respect boundaries and self-control were more likely to show the same compassion, guilt, and responsibility for their actions.

Narcissism can also be seen in parents who treat children like objects of praise or watch them through their eyes, ultimately denying and disempowering them by teaching children that they are just objects, causing the child who is narcissistic to see the world as a collection of objects to be put at their possession, but also believing that they are very significant. In this scenario it is possible to have the simultaneous "overvaluation" in addition to "neglect" that causes an unhealthy narcissism within a child. the parent may overvalue the child's worthiness however, they can create a feelings of inadequacy because they do not provide children with more consistent information that affirms who they are as human beings.

This is due to the fact that the child who is narcissistic is viewed by society as "great" and isn't given the real-world perspective regarding this kind of feedback. It makes it more difficult for the child, instead of as a person with three dimensions to become a prize. It also instills a amount in entitlement for children by thereby instilling in the children that they are entitled to things they did not earn.

As this parental overvaluation is not balanced by acceptance of the flawed worthiness of the child, the child is likely to develop a sense grandeur that oscillates between feelings of unworthiness and a inflated ego, which is the narcissism that is not having a positive self-image (De Lisle 2015). In spite of a healthy self-esteem and self acceptance, it can also cause a child to place a high value on some aspect over another, like appearance, academic performance or a different ability.

However, parents are not the sole ones accountable for their children's growth of narcissism. Fortunately, there are many parents of narcissistic children who provide a nurturing and safe environment that their child. This is the place where we have to know the source of genetic predispositions within families. Twin studies have revealed that a universal heritable, genetically inherited character is the narcissism (Livesley and. and others 1993). There's also a neurological and biological perspective that helps us to discover how someone who has NPD the brain of those with no NPD.

Studies have shown that in people who are narcissistic, there are neurological disorders that are linked to empathy and compassion that is crucial to be aware of as psychopaths might have brain disorders as well. psychopaths do not just display emotional disorders, but they also display anomalies in the growth of prosocial emotions, such as regret as well as moral thinking (Schulze)

Although every hypothesis is valid and has its own unique set of proofs, I want to stress that the cause of NPD is not completely evident to clinicians. It is possible that the solution is much more complex than any theory. Psychopathology is, to my mind usually caused through a connection between genetic predisposition and the environment. There are also elements of multiculturalism that, in certain countries, can make certain disorders more likely than others , or manifest differently depending on the context.

We must be aware that there are factors of protection and risk-factors that determine the extent to which narcissism develops into a full personality disorder and how it manifests within the person. In general, it's not about food vs nature and more of a combination of both diet and nature-the majority of disorders result from the effects of the connection between the biology and environment, not the latter. The factors that contribute to this include a the strength of your connections to the social world access to treatment or medication as well as upbringing, religious beliefs as well as community, media and many other interactions outside of the family unit , such as sexual assault, bullying or experiencing abuse, and other traumas that could contribute to the weakening or strengthening of the likelihood of pathology.

Simply put Narcissists can be created in a variety of ways. They can be born from various environments. Through the interaction of the natural environment and biology the narcissism of their personality can develop. I've known Narcissists of all backgrounds including traumatized as being overvalued, that were raised with a sense of entitlement. their parents instilled an unwholesome belief in entitlement. It's crucial to recognize that narcissists could have a range of backgrounds, and that this connection between the biological predisposition of a person and their surroundings typically leads to psychopathology.

While survivors can't be 100% certain about the cause of their partner's NPD or their spouse, what they are certain about is that having an NPD partner could be extremely harmful and destructive due to their inability to understand and exploitation. I am able to answer the questions "why"? and "how? and "how?" "The responsibility that blames the victim, not the abuser can cause confusion. Simply because someone has disabilities doesn't mean that they aren't a victim of abuse or that they're not accountable for their abuse or the violence they commit doesn't harm the victim.

Absolutely not. Anyone with a condition and isn't seeking professional help. If you are unable to modify behavior that causes harm to others, and persists in using the condition as a reason for abusers, they could be blamed for their actions. We should certainly be aware that the person we abused may have suffered trauma and hurt, but we shouldn't let our sympathy make us blind to the need to be able to show our self-compassion and self-care our top priority to be able to separate from them when they're not able to change or receive assistance, which most narcissists can't.

In this kind of unidirectional relationship, you'll eventually be treated as a source of admiration, love or attention, as well as whatever else they might require at any given moment This is the kind of thing Otto Fenichel (1945) calls an element from "narcissistic supplies." If you are in an intimate relationship with someone who is a narcissist, take care because the person you think you are is always charming and distinct from the true self , that you could fall victim. A cognitive dissonance leads to an emotional predator falling in love is amplified due to the mask that is shown in the public eye by the Narcissist. The narcissist's personality is determined by where the person falls within the continuum in their relationship, a connection with a narcissist usually involves an element of emotional, psychological and in some instances sexual and physical violence.

Chapter 13: The Gaslight Law in The Workplace

Narcissists tend to be bullies, and they love being bullies. If you work with a narcissist colleague at work, you'll see that they enjoy the way they bully other people. They also will assume the role of your superior even when they're not. They may ask you to complete tasks that are not in the pay scale of your job. They may ask you to begin filling out forms that will allow you to be acknowledged certified public accountant. Therefore, they employ different methods to intimidate you. They may even shout at you. They may suggest you commit a crime that you've never done. They may lie about your actions. They may yell at you. They could use insults against you. They could steal things from you. They may even talk about you in private. They could get your lunch out of the fridge, and when you find them, they'll inform you that it's not your lunch.

Sabotage your decks

They may sabotage your decks. If you have a coworker with a personality disorder at your work environment, there is a good chance that you'll be subject to lots of harassment. In addition, the majority of narcissists tend to harass others sexually. Because they are not compassionate towards other people and always seek to take advantage of others.

They don't consider others as valued members of the community who are entitled to feelings. These men are obsessed with exploring the opinions of others with regard to sexual harassment, and they're more likely to be involved in it. There is a connection between narcissism, sexual harassment and narcissism it has been reported in media several times, revealing that individuals working for major companies and music industry bosses have been involved by sexual assault. If you're in a workplace in which someone is exploiting others at work and making remarks about what they look like or the way their bodies look or shaming others and making comments about their appearance, then they're narcissist individuals.

Use you to their advantage to make money for themselves

Narcissists are known to take advantage of others to their advantage in order that they can boost their self-esteem, especially when they hold an authority position and even if not, they're likely to harass people. If you have a coworker who exhibits these characteristics, you will see them constantly pushing your ego to the point they want to be able to see their whole self. So long as you keep playing the game, they'll be on great relations with you. However, when you start to create them, they'll feel let down by your actions. Once they discover that you've identified them, they'll be on the road to war.

A person who is a narcissist can be in one place and then off the next. There isn't any middle ground because they either love or are angry with you. You either don't bother them or attempt to bring you down. They may be friends one day, but when they realize that you experience an unlucky day and cannot support their extravagant idea of who they are or when they believe that you're getting some recognition within the organization, they'll be frightened of your actions. If you begin getting ahead of the Superior in the company someone who has a narcissist personality within the company will view it as threat. Therefore, if there is a time when Power or their perception of authority over you or the other person has been undermined If you do, you'll reveal the dark side of their personality.

Monopolize conversations

People who have high narcissist tendencies have a tendency to dominate conversations as they are attracted to attention. They often boast about their work achievements. They're so inefficient and it is evident clearly, yet they would like you to believe they're highly efficient and valued in the business. They constantly boast about what they did or didn't do. They might meet with the CEO in the parking lot however, when they come back the next day for work, and they'll begin talking about how they had dinner at the table with the CEO and that the CEO has decided to name their child an identity as their coworker. They will exaggerate their status and want you to believe them. They want you to fall into their fantasy world.

They dominate conversations. They attempt to take advantage of every person who work in the office. Their goal lies in being who is in the middle. The one who is easily upset, and the one who is putting everyone with on eggshells, and do your best to not accept their opinions. If you're engaged in an argument, they'll be present and attempt to divert conversations to themselves. They will also proclaim their worth within the company to cover their own security. Anyone who is able to confess that he did not take a step and apologizes straight away is someone who has integrity, and is entirely acceptable.

If you're working with a narcissist work or someone who has these traits of a narcissist You will observe that when they make errors and don't even admit they did it. In fact, they'll come up with every excuse they can think of to blame others for an action that didn't work out or wasn't accomplished.

They are unwilling to accept responsibility; instead, they make fun of everyone in the room , and most of the time, they pick the one who doesn't challenge against them. They'll lie about their own mistakes and blame it upon someone at work whom they believe won't be able to fight back or they believe is likely to back down.

This is why it's crucial to establish limits, and that you discover ways to keep narcotics individuals at bay. However, this is a major aspect in the whole process. They are unable to admit their humanity since they've spent so much time dominating other people's attention and spending so much time justifying their actions. When it comes to them finally admitting they've committed mistakes, they'll not admit to it.

Give credit to your work

One of the most challenging aspects of the people they are often claim credit for the work you've done. They're the self-centered person who is sitting at home and ignoring you, asking for details, and then asking you what you've accomplished on the project and obtaining all the details. They might even offer to buy coffee for you and encourage you to will complete the task and to be credited for the project. This is an indication of their inability to be concerned about others in a genuine way. Their goal is to keep control over those they work with. They want to manipulate, control and control other people, therefore, when working with a narcissist you'll be unable to continue doing this.

There is evidence that those who have narcissist characteristics have a tendency to exploit others and lack empathy for others and try to take the credit for other people's work. If you've experienced this, you'll notice that it's one of your most challenging things that can happen to you. You are the kind that attends work every day and strives to do your best performance at work, and strives to grow and climb to the top of to the top of corporate ranks. However, along the way you are constantly interacting people with narcissistic tendencies and those who lie and gaslights, who is a bully, who undermines your work, and then exploits you and take your job.

Conclusion

Gaslighting is a type of psychological manipulation performed by someone who aims to create doubt in the mind of a person or group of people by restraining their perception, memory or even their health. Gaslighting employs denial or misdirection, inconsistent behavior, and deceit to undermine the victim and undermine the beliefs that the person who is victimized. The circumstances vary from the disbelief of the abuser of the fact that violent incidents in the past were the cause to the investigation conducted by the abuser into bizarre circumstances to destabilize the victim.

Gaslighting is an act of psychological manipulation in which the victim continuously manipulates the circumstances to question his memories and beliefs. Gaslighting is an act of abuse which is nefarious. The victim is deprived of their very instincts that they've relied upon throughout their lives and makes them in complete obscurity about anything. Gaslighting is a sure way that victims will believe everything the perpetrators say about their experience. Most other forms of physical and emotional abuse are preceded by the gaslighting because the victim is more susceptible to abuse in other circumstances.

Many gaslighting methods are available that make it difficult to detect gaslighting. Gaslights are employed to conceal the truth that the perpetrator doesn't want the victim to know. Men or women can continue the use of gas in a way that is harmful.

The gassing technique of withholding where the victim appears to be unaware or indifferent, and refuses to talk about his thoughts. Gaslighting techniques are employed to for the person to question his thoughts, feelings as well as his memories and behavior. Most often, the victim is afraid to speak up about a topic because they fear they're in the wrong place or don't comprehend the issue.

The most harmful gas lighters can create circumstances for the usage of gas lamps. A good example is to remove keys of the victim from where they are always to make the victim believe they've done something wrong. Helping the victim locate keys that are difficult to remember.

www.ingramcontent.com/pod-product-compliance
Lightning Source LLC
Chambersburg PA
CBHW060334030426
42336CB00011B/1342